HOW TO STAY SOBER

Recovery Without Religion

James Christopher

PROMETHEUS BOOKS
Buffalo, New York

91 90 89   4 3

Library of Congress Cataloging-in-Publication Data

Christopher, James, 1942–
    How to stay sober.

    Bibliography: p.
    1. Alcoholics—Rehabilitation.   I. Title.
HV5276.C57   1988   362.2'928   88-1139
ISBN 0-87975-438-9 (Cloth)
ISBN 0-87975-457-5 (Paper)

Contents

Dedication

Dying from the elements in doorways of condemned buildings during eastern city winters, curled up near heaps of refuse in sunny California's alleyways, they are legion.

Poems are written, songs composed, jokes circulated; judgments, warnings, "but for the grace of God," and "walk a mile in his shoes" are recited.

Human beings give up and literally have nothing to live for but the next drink, cells damaged beyond restoration. The caretakers of society routinely pull sheets over forgotten faces and midnight missions ready next week's nameless, offering false assurances of "life after life." But there are only so many vacant seats.

Herein is a tribute to those for whom the bell tolls, clanging loudly to drown out the rattle of money changing hands, exacerbated by the perpetuation of misinformation, quelling the softer sounds of egos remaining intact and the rustle of thriving vested interests. For them it is too late. They were and are "guilty" of a physiological disease advanced beyond recall.

Their lives have become destruction incarnate, moral guilt is heaped upon their weary backs; spit in their faces mingled with tears has provided preachers and comedians with material for centuries.

To them and to the future of alcoholism research I dedicate this book.

Foreword
by Gerald A. Larue

Many, if not most, of us are hooked on mood-changing chemicals Fortunately, those that most of us use are not particularly harmfu¹ to ourselves or to society. Some need that first cup of coffee to begin the day; others want a cup of tea in the afternoon. These particular mood-changers are pick-me-ups that permit us to pause or break routine. They may help to carry us through daily stresses. On the index charts, caffeine addiction is on the low side of addictability. At the other extreme are the hard drugs, such as heroin, cocaine, barbiturates, and amphetamines. Then comes alcohoı.

Alcohol is a mood-changer that can become an addiction. Alcoholism is sometimes labeled the disease of denial, because of misconceptions about what alcoholism is ("I'm not an alcoholic, I go to work everyday" or "I just have a few drinks in the evening to relax") and who it affects ("I'm not a bum on skid row"). Alcoholism has been called an "equal opportunity" disease; it touches people from all socio-economic classes, all races, all ethnic groups, all ages, all religious backgrounds. It affects the individual alcoholic and his or her family and work, as well as the safety and welfare of society in general.

Any responsible therapist dealing with alcoholics seeking sobriety will be familiar with the issues considered in this important book. The desperate addict will have been exposed to all sorts of treatment by so-called experts, many of whom know about alcoholism from one-day courses on the subject or from reading books by other so-called experts. He or she will have experienced medicinal (drug) therapy, group therapy, behavioral modification therapy, membership in Alcoholics Anonymous, and so on. For some persons, one or more of these treatment patterns seem to work; for others, they fail.

Jim Christopher is an alcoholic—a sober alcoholic, but an alcoholic nevertheless. It is really unimportant for us to know how he became addicted—whether he went through the commonly accepted addiction model, starting with occasional use, passing through regular use to mental dependency, and finally reaching chemical dependency. What matters is that he is an alcoholic and that, out of his own pain and need, he has developed a program that offers hope and a means of control for alcoholism.

One of the most popular and most highly recommended patterns of treatment is the one used by Alcoholics Anonymous. As anyone who has engaged in treatment of alcoholics will know, there are those who simply do not, cannot, and will not accept the notion of surrendering oneself or one's life to a "Higher Power," no matter how it is defined. These persons are the skeptics, the nonbelievers, the questioners, and those who simply do not want to substitute an addiction to one "power" (alcohol) for submission to another. They want self-control. They want to be in charge of their own lives.

Jim Christopher's Secular Sobriety Groups offer the alcoholic self-control. There is no miraculous outside wonder-working power included in this program. The addict is provided with a day-by-day means of handling alcoholism. When two or three secular sobrietists gather together, they can offer support and encouragement to one another. There is no magic here and the program works.

This book is written for alcoholics. It is also a tool for therapists and counselors who can put copies into the hands of those for whom traditional faith systems are ineffective. It can be the basis for establishing Secular Sobriety Groups in hospitals, counseling centers and, indeed, wherever there is a need.

There is within each of us an instinctual drive to live. We want to live well, to be in control of our lives. Because we are social creatures, we want others to live and live well too. This book makes an important contribution to prolonging and enhancing the lives of alcoholics, to enriching the lives of their families and loved ones, and to protecting the lives of those who become the victims of alcoholics who drink and drive. Responsible sobriety, under personal control, is the key.

Introduction

For me it all started with a couple of cold beers on a hot Texas afternoon, driving home, dreamily tired, feeling good. I was young with a job well done under my belt and my old Chevy whizzed along magnificently. Unsuspecting, I had introduced alcohol into a body that could not process the drug as ninety percent of the world's bodies could. I unknowingly joined my brothers and sisters in the ten percent category, beginning the hidden, insidious, progressive disease of alcoholism.

With no more evil intent than a cancer victim has, and no more or less emotionally mature than any nonalcoholic, I entered into agony.

Fellow Texans drank their beers, sometimes getting drunk, sometimes not. Physiologically, I gradually began to part company with my nonalcoholic friends, internally following a decidedly different path. As my physical disease rendered me more and more a helpless addict, my personality became distorted, my reasoning powers compromised, my concepts and feelings literally absorbed in alcohol.

During seventeen years of active addiction to alcohol, I often drank to blackout/passout levels on a nearly daily basis. High blood pressure caused broken vessels on my no-longer-rosy cheeks. My promises and commitments to myself and others became impossible to keep. And so it went.

Two hard hats had become angered by my ramblings. I was convinced they were going to kill me. Struggling off the bar stool, stumbling toward some friendlier faces, I pleaded for protection. Shortly after a forgotten conversation, I ran out of the bar onto a rubbery-looking pavement. As if in a nightmare, I fell, crying and screaming, onto the hard, cold, non-rubber street.

I somehow got to my feet, wiping the blood and tears from my face, and ran, weaving my way to my home about a block away. Throwing myself against a tree at the rear entrance of my duplex, I tore down my pants to urinate and collapsed in an alcoholic stupor, "sleeping" till daybreak.

This was one of many incidents leading up to my sobriety date of April 24, 1978. I have not had a drink since.

As a fortunate human being with an arrested but permanent disease, I no longer have the option of blowing away a bad day or celebrating a great day with liquor or other mind-altering drugs. My nonalcoholic friends have this option, not because they are any more emotionally stable than I am, but because they are in the aforementioned ninety-percent league.

Having experienced addiction to mind-altering drugs, we alcoholics are permanently changed, physiologically.

We should always be aware of and accept our disease. Unlike nonalcoholics, who can walk away from booze after achieving a pleasurable buzz, high, or drunk, we cannot escape. We must, out of life-and-death necessity, choose alternatives to chemicals for easing life's burdens or highlighting its pleasures.

If we think we can marry Millie or Teddy, move to a quiet suburb, and put alcoholism out of our minds, we are rejecting our salvation from active addiction.

If we trust in the intercession of a mythical mystical power, odds are that irrational beliefs will be sorely tested. Life experiences can, on a not-so-fine day, push into the background a weakened grasp of reality, clouded by religion, and possibly resurrect our dormant addiction. We can lose our faith; we need not lose our sobriety.

The victims of child abuse, rape, the Vietnam war, the Holocaust, and other horrors—although often restored to productiveness and health—know whence I speak when I say that an integral part of one's being is a lifelong awareness and acceptance of that which cannot and should not be denied, even though it is no longer an active reality. The alcoholic not only cannot forget, but *must* not forget. In my lifelong daily recovery process I glance back; I do not have to stare.

Sobriety as the priority in our lives enables us to continue living and allows us a relative handle on reality.

Science has established that alcoholism is a physiological disease predetermined by heredity. Alcohol is a selectively physically addictive drug; the majority of users and even abusers do not become physically addicted to alcohol. Personality, psychology, emotional responses, and environment do not bring about physical addiction. All kinds of persons are nonalcoholics. All kinds of persons are alcoholics.

Nonalcoholics do not become physiologically addicted to alcohol simply because their bodies process it differently than do the bodies of alcoholics.

The evidence is strong that there is no such thing as an "alcoholic personality." J. H. P. Willis, a consultant psychiatrist at Guy's Hospital and King's College Hospital in London, has studied drug abuse and dependence. He writes:

Very often it appears that speculation and non-verifiable assertion have been considerably mixed together when various authorities have tried to explain the nature of addiction. A good example of this is found in the "psychosocial" approach to addiction. In this there appears to be a general hypothesis that people can become addicted to drugs as a result of a confluence of factors in which social and psychological forces operate forcefully within the individual, as it were, driving him inexorably toward being a drug addict. This has led to an enormous amount of speculation, which has found perhaps its most absurd expression in the notion put forward by a number of psychologists and psychiatrists that there is a special type of personality which is, as it were, addiction-prone. Unfortunately, however, no one has ever been able to substantiate this claim in any credible way.[1]

In his book, *The Natural History of Alcoholism,* George E. Vaillant, a professor of psychiatry at Dartmouth Medical School, writes:

Far more surprising, most future alcoholics do not appear different from future asymptomatic drinkers in terms of premorbid psychological stability. However, not until several prospective studies were available, could such a hypothesis be seriously entertained. It was difficult to conceive that the "alcoholic personality" might be secondary to the disorder, alcoholism. It was difficult to discard the illusion that alcohol serves as a successful self-medication for unhappy, diffident people. In actual fact, however, alcohol in high doses is the very opposite of a tranquilizer.

In dismissing unhappy childhoods, membership in multiproblem families, depression, and anxiety from major etiological consideration, I do not wish to say that these factors are of no importance in alcoholism. These factors will make any chronic disease worse. I simply wish to underscore that in a prospective design, when other more salient variables like culture and familial alcoholism per se were controlled, then premorbid family and personality instability no longer made a statistical contribution to the risk of alcoholism. Thus, Core City subjects with an alcoholic parent but with an otherwise stable family were *five* times as likely to develop alcoholism as were subjects from clearly multiproblem families without an alcoholic parent.

In retrospect, individuals often rationalized their slowly developing loss of control over alcohol use by citing past psychological trauma. Prospectively studied, however, abuse of alcohol usually predated the alleged trauma, and reactive alcohol abuse was rarely observed to be a cause of alcohol dependence. . . . In other words, a difficult life was rarely a major reason why someone developed alcohol dependence.

In summary, alcoholics often come from broken homes because their parents abused alcohol, not because broken homes cause alcoholism; and alcoholics are selectively personality-disordered as a consequence, not as a cause, of their alcohol abuse. Although the conscience may be soluble in alcohol, heavy alcohol use does not relieve anxiety and depression as much as alcohol abuse induces depression and anxiety.[2]

James R. Milam and Katherine Ketcham, authors of *Under the Influence—A Guide to the Myths and Realities of Alcoholism*, write:

The alcoholic starts drinking the same ways and for the same reasons the nonalcoholic starts drinking. He drinks to gain the effects of alcohol—to feel euphoric, stimulated, relaxed, or intoxicated. Sometimes he drinks to ease his frustrations; other times he drinks to put himself in a good mood. If he is tense, he may drink more than usual in an effort to unwind and get his mind off his troubles; if shy, he may drink to gain confidence; if extroverted, he may drink because he likes the company of other drinkers.

The alcoholic, like the nonalcoholic, is influenced in the way he drinks, where he drinks, how much, and how often he drinks by numerous psychological, social, or cultural factors. He may start drinking to impress his girl friend, to prove he is not afraid of his parent's disapproval, or because he is taunted into it by his friends. He may drink regularly because alcohol makes him laugh and forget his troubles or because he feels self-assured after a few drinks. If his wife has a cocktail every night, he may drink to keep her company. If his coworkers are heavy drinkers, he may learn to drink heavily.

Again like the nonalcoholic, the alcoholic learns to drink a variety of alcoholic beverages, and he develops preferences among beers, wines, and liquors. He learns how much and how fast people ordinarily drink on various occasions, and he learns how well he can "hold his liquor," how much it takes for him to feel good, to get high, or to get drunk.

Alcoholics as well as nonalcoholics may change their drinking habits because of life changes: death of a loved one, divorce, loss of a job. Loneliness, depression, fears and insecurities may also affect the way a person drinks. *The point is that none of these psychological or social factors are unique to either the alcoholic or nonalcoholic. Members of both groups drink together for the same reasons and with the same reinforcement by alcohol's stimulating and energizing effects.* The same variety of personality traits is found in both groups. Earlier advocates of an "alcoholic personality" have abandoned this hypothesis, and the theory of an "addictive personality" has also been discredited by lack of supportive evidence.[3]

When we disappoint ourselves, behaving in a manner that causes anxiety, guilt, or fear, we are hurt, angered, or frightened, yet we alcoholics must respect our arrested disease and remain sober. We must reach higher in creative ways, higher perhaps than if we were nonalcoholics. It is solely up to us to individually give our lives meaning.

An alcoholic may or may not be emotionally stable and able to cope psychologically with life's problems when the physiological addiction sets in. His pre-addiction emotional make-up becomes altered, warped, and distorted. Only in sobriety—recovery—does the alcoholic experience his or her true personality, character, and ethics.

In early sobriety and with equal fervor throughout the remainder of an alcoholic's life, the priority must be to control the permanent disease of alcoholism. Alcoholism will not go away—ever. Sobriety, the only antidote to alcoholism, does not have to go away either—ever.

The recovery process is obviously lifelong, as there is no known cure for alcoholism. And the phenomenon of "cross tolerance"—that is, the crossover addiction from alcohol to other mind-altering drugs—has been well-established.

Arresting addiction through conscious choice puts the recovered alcoholic into the same arena as those who, through conscious choice, can use or abuse alcohol and have only fleeting annoyance or psychological pain to show for it.

The true alcoholic's chances of recovery are quite remote. We alcoholics must live creatively in sobriety on life's terms, lifelong, *no matter what*. Whether we continually find peace in acceptance of who and what we are or are not is secondary to keeping our disease at bay, arrested, inactive throughout our lives.

This can be (and often is) a challenging and dynamically creative adventure.

1 Can Sober Alcoholics Ever Drink Again?

A great man once said "I have a dream." Dr. Martin Luther King's words touched our hearts and also made a great deal of sense. Although his struggle for civil rights cost him his life, the dream lives on through those who believe that freedom from racism and oppression are noble goals.

To end the possibility of nuclear war by developing a cooperative "global mentality," to achieve nuclear disarmament, eradicate hunger, and conquer disease are all monumental challenges, pinnacles toward which humanity aspires.

And then there are those who experiment with alcoholics in an attempt to "normalize" or "modify" their drinking behavior. The magnitude of their work is outweighed only by the multitude of grants allotted it. Countless alcoholics have died in the process. I participated in one such experiment after having spent years in "traditional" therapy.

My personal parade of shrinks includes a guy who asked his patients to give him a frog upon completion of their therapy. You read correctly. He had shelf upon shelf of ceramic frogs, cloth frogs, stuffed frogs, small frogs, large frogs, and everything in between. In presenting him with a frog, one symbolically gave up frogdom, thereby acknowledging one's new self to be a prince or princess.

When I once cancelled a $200 weekend "intensive" because of a bad case of stomach flu, one well-known therapist/author conveyed to me, via his secretary, that I "still owed the money (although somewhat smaller payments would be acceptable)" and that I was to "think of it in the same way one would when committed to buying a theater ticket." After all, this was a busy man, flying from New York to Los Angeles and back to New York for bi-coastal "intensives," weekend "marathons." This was the big time; dare I question it?

An elderly psychologist, approaching life problems "didactically as well as eclectically," had me lie nude upon her couch occasionally in order to reveal my "body language."

Another taught me not to say yes when I really wanted to say no, and informed me at the end of my series of treatments that if I was an alcoholic, with all the current challenges in my life, "*everyone* must be alcoholic."

Yet another doctor, a psychiatrist, gave me various mood medications that made me feel as though I were wearing a football helmet. He put me on lithium, stuck me with needles (to draw blood lithium levels), and would look away from me when I tried to make eye contact.

In one of my most colorful therapy groups the psychiatrist instructed us to revert to childhood and gave us water guns and plastic toys. And for lunch, having paired off in twos, we had to feed our partners fried chicken and mashed potatoes with one hand behind our backs, using no fork or spoon. This, it was explained, developed trust and intimacy-potential. We were allowed to visit the toilet by ourselves.

So, back in the good old seventies, when I heard about the now infamous Rand Report, I drove my car right up to the front steps of the Rand Corporation in Santa Monica, California, hopeful in my alcoholic denial. I gingerly stepped into the main lobby and secured my very own copy of the report from one of the think tank's employees.

I raced home and read and re-read the good parts. Yep, alcoholics—and by then I knew I was one—could drink again. A few days later I spoke to one of the authors of this research, eager to change my life. After I told him that I had a long history of problem drinking and that I was an alcoholic, he said "Yes, you people just have to learn not to drink so much."

Well, I couldn't have agreed more. I asked this clever chap if he could recommend a doctor in the field of behavior modification for alcoholics. He could indeed. I called and set my first appointment. "Zowie! At long last," I thought, "I'll be able to control and enjoy my drinking, like everyone else." Denial often takes alcoholics to strange places and I headed several miles away to a small neighboring town.

The clinic looked very official, very scientific. I was greeted by a cheery receptionist and handed a number of forms to fill out. The psychologist then joined me for an initial evaluation. I was honest at this juncture about my drinking history, as the preceding years of addictive drinking had pretty much beaten me down. I told the good doctor that Alcoholics Anonymous had been a disappointment for me, with its narrow viewpoints and religious stance. He fully agreed and even joked with me, repeating A.A. slogans like "Keep coming back," "Put the plug in the jug," etc. I just knew I'd hit pay dirt and arrived "home." Doc explained that he was a "maverick," that his methods were sometimes considered controversial, and that treatment would be expensive. I was an average-income kind of guy, but was willing to continue to sacrifice as I had for years, working with various therapies and therapists to determine why I began drinking.

Given my alcohol history, Doc said, the chances that I could modify my drinking behavior were "fifty-fifty."

After I filled out more forms, he took me on a tour of the clinic, and was I in for a treat! A large room at the rear had been turned into a friendly neighborhood tavern, complete with beer signs on the wall behind the padded bar, bright plastic bar stools, and a chrome foot-railing. Doc explained that I was to come back at a later date, driven by a friend, for my very own "drunk night."

Also included in my tour was a visit to a high-tech room

filled with state-of-the-art video equipment hooked up to cameras strategically placed throughout the bar. Alongside the bar sat an elaborate breathalyzer device, into which I was to blow periodically on "drunk night."

All this would eventually teach me how to "not hurt" myself on nights of moderate drinking and how to experience a pleasant "high" with the consumption of less alcohol. So safe was this level, I was told, that after my initial "drunk night" (an experience that Doc assured me I'd never again have to go through, at least not in his simulated tavern) I would not require a friend to drive me home. On nights of moderate drinking I could safely drive myself home after sitting in the clinic until the level of alcohol in my blood dropped sufficiently. "Drunk night," he explained, was to include my being videotaped from various angles during the proceedings, which would last approximately four hours. The tapes would be played back to me prior to my moderation-learning sessions. This was to shame me into shaping up. When "drunk night" arrived, I traveled to the clinic by bus. I had arranged for a good friend to come by for me at about 9 P.M.

The doctor had asked in advance my choice of alcoholic beverage for the evening. I had selected what was then my favorite: very dry vodka martinis. All was set when I confidently stepped into the fake bar. The doctor and a young assistant acted as hosts/ bartenders, serving up chilled martinis as fast as I could put them away; olives were included. At various intervals I was instructed to blow into a tube attached to the breathalyzer. I quickly passed the giddy-bright-chatty stage (I told my doctor he was fat) and moved right into the more depressed stage of my drinking. I began to blubber, pounding on the bar. I got off the barstool, seeing double, and stumbled over a couch, where I proceeded to throw up into a large plastic pail they had provided for me. I was then wrapped in a light blanket and allowed to pass out until my friend arrived to walk me to his station wagon, with the help of Doc and his assistant.

A few days later I sat in the "screening room" at the clinic, viewing my "drunk night" antics. Although seeing myself in such humiliating circumstances made me feel bad about my behavior, I also remember thinking that all this seemed a bit crazy, as if I were participating in some surreal tragicomedy. And I felt sorry for myself.

I became, as the weeks passed, a model patient, sincerely learn ing my level of moderation and, while drinking at home, using a measuring cup as I'd been taught. I drank every day and night (moderately, of course). I had to log my drinking behavior and bring the information with me to each session at the clinic. A chart made from this information showed marked "progress" as I drank moderately or heavily most nights, and went out of control relatively few nights.

After numerous sessions and additional training in relaxation techniques, I was discharged and wished good luck.

It's common for alcoholics to experience some periods of moderate alcohol intake. I didn't know this at the time and dutifully continued to regulate the amounts with my plastic measuring cup.

It was only a matter of weeks until I was again "off and running." The cravings had been increasing; the chemical need was back in full force.

Alcoholism continues. Theories regarding alcoholism come and go. Some alcoholism professionals look for *why*, some for *why not*. Meanwhile, we alcoholics have the option to choose sobriety: as one recovering alcoholic put it, "My drinker broke." Personally, I wouldn't trade my years of sobriety for any pill or innovation that would involve the reintroduction of booze back into my body. And for me, the answer to the question, "Can sober alcoholics ever drink again?" is an emphatic *no*.

2 A.A. and Beyond: Sobriety Without Superstition

There are an estimated sixty million unchurched citizens in this country today and, based on statistics regarding the general population, approximately six million of these are alcoholics.

Since its inception in 1935, Alcoholics Anonymous has helped legions of individuals recover from alcoholism; A.A. retains no records but claims a recovery rate of seventy-five percent. Only five percent of this nation's ten-to-fifteen million problem drinkers (approximately 500,000 to 750,000) are helped by A.A.

What about the remaining nine-and-one-half million to fourteen-and-a-quarter million alcoholics who aren't "A.A.ers"? Could *some* of them be atheists, agnostics, secular humanists, deists, pantheists, or free thinkers who rely on humankind's collective scientific knowledge to date and cannot, in good conscience, accept A.A.'s concept of an intervening God or "Higher Power" in their lives?

Although A.A. supposedly welcomes for membership anyone with a desire to stop drinking, their "Big Book" states: "The alcoholic at certain times has no effective mental defense against the first drink. Except in a few rare cases, neither he nor any other human being can provide such a defense. His defense must come from a Higher Power."

A.A. does reach religious persons, especially during this era of religiosity, and many are helped, *if* they buy A.A.'s rigid party line of turning their will and lives over to the care of God "as they understand Him."

A.A. has "come of age" in some respects. It now offers meetings accessible to the physically disabled. (Although I recall suggesting this to the Los Angeles Central Office a number of years ago and having my request turned down. The reply: "You just concern yourself with staying sober; if disabled folks want sobriety badly enough, they'll find a way to get here.")

A.A. now holds meetings in Spanish and lists non-smokers meetings in its local directories.

A.A. now officially recognizes lesbian and gay meetings, although I recall that at one time, gay meetings had to be held under a name other then A.A.—even though they adhered to A.A. principles and used materials purchased from A.A.'s central office. I also recall a long-sober lesbian alcoholic who tearfully related her story: She'd worked many years for the A.A. cause and one day overheard, in her local central office, insensitive remarks about lesbians and gays not being wanted in the general fellowship of A.A. Since, unfortunately, her sobriety was based upon A.A. and God as her higher power, her world was shattered and she reverted to alcoholism for a time. Fortunately, she has now made it back to sobriety.

A.A. now officially recognizes agnostics and atheists in meetings —again, after many years of resistance. In these controversial meetings the Lord's Prayer is deleted and a secularized, non-mystical higher power is used, such as the universe, the A.A. group, a tree, a walrus, etc. Obviously the concept of a higher power becomes meaningless. Being inspired by the A.A. group or being in awe of the natural universe is one thing; expecting another human being (much less a walrus) to keep one sober is quite another.

As the old saying goes: "If it waddles like a duck and quacks like a duck, it probably is a duck." A.A. was founded over fifty years ago on the religious concept of a higher power or "God as you understand Him." The Big Book of Alcoholics Anonymous also stresses that agnostics will eventually "come to believe." Fiesty free thinkers within the membership of A.A.—a membership supposedly requiring only "an honest desire to stop drinking"—

continue to use the group's official statement of purpose at secularized meetings. This is a real step forward within A.A. for answering the needs of nonreligious persons. However, the shadow of religion looms in the background, whereas autonomous secular groups with no ties to A.A. could answer the needs of any free-thinking alcoholic who desires a secular support group to deal with a very human affliction without the crutches of faith healing and higher powers.

But not all free thinkers are fiesty and aggressive. Fearfully equating A.A. with sobriety, many nonbelievers keep their opinions to themselves, experience alienation and eventually leave the "fellowship."

In its official Big Book and in other A.A. materials, alcoholics are presented as childlike personalities, emotional cripples explaining in their own words *why* they became alcholics. This increases their guilt and shame, and reduces their chances of recovery. Enter the Higher Power, popularly nicknamed "H.P."

When their jobs are done, most, if not all, alcoholism treatment programs and courts of law trot the newly sober alcoholics off to be indoctrinated with A.A.'s twelve-step theology within the secular setting of a hospital or clinic. Many newly sober alcoholics come to A.A. not through a court order or an alcoholism treatment program, but simply because they seek the fellowship and support of other sober alcoholics and find that traditional A.A., complete with H.P., is often all there is.

Again, what about free thinkers? Must we give up our identities and our free-thought processes and develop faith in a higher power to stay sober? Obviously not. Obvious to me now, several years after gaining a less-robotic foothold on my sobriety. But not so obvious in the beginning—especially during the first few days, weeks, months, and through the first year of my sobriety.

Unless driven away by dogma (usually to an eventual alcoholic death, I might add), newly sober alcoholics, delicately hanging onto their fragile lives, are ready to consider *any* philosophy, religion, or support. I call this the grateful syndrome. Alcoholics will accept anything during this period, as sobriety must be the alcoholic's priority.

Although sobriety must *remain* the alcoholic's priority lifelong, we alcoholics need not be intimidated into mindlessness as the price for staying sober.

I remember questioning things at A.A. meetings in my early sobriety: "What is 'God's will'? How do nontheists, Jews, and Buddhists feel about saying the Lord's Prayer?" One longtime A.A. member simply said, "Shut up!" Another answered, "Your best thinking got you here," meaning if you "think"—that is, if you question A.A. dogma—it really means that you want to drink. Yet another said, "If those heretics truly want to stay sober, they'll join hands and say the Lord's Prayer, if they know what's good for 'em!"

These attitudes remain, I suspect, because of the remnant moral stigma regarding alcoholism, and the "one way" concept of religionists.

An only child reared in Texas by Baptist parents, I was carefully taught to fear God and to feel enormous guilt for many "sins." I took religious teachings to heart and mind.

My father was an alcoholic. Just as I will never forget how to ride a bicycle, I'll always have the undercurrent of addiction etched in my psyche.

I came to my position of unbelief gradually, as a sober alcoholic. However, my early sobriety was the most vulnerable period of my life and I, like so many others in A.A., felt intimidated, hesitant, and terrified to challenge the group lest I lose my precious sobriety. In these precarious early stages, a moment of rational thought about the supernatural foundations of sobriety based on religion could cause a complete reversal of progress.

I remember a terrifying moment at an A.A. meeting in my early sobriety when I suddenly thought, "What if this God *wants* me to drink?"

Stretching my legs during the coffee break, I collided with another anonymous alcoholic, causing the contents in the styrofoam cup I was carrying to slosh out suddenly.

"Oh, God," he said, "H.P. *is* watching over us, isn't He!" This fellow's interpretation of the incident: Because the coffee did not spill on us but rather landed harmlessly on the floor, we'd been protected and spared from wetness (sparrows, eat your hearts out) by the Higher Power. If the liquid had drenched us, I feel reasonably certain my friend would have seen it as God's will.

Being wrapped in the swaddling clothes of cult care can be comforting as long as one doesn't stray from the "protection" of the A.A. party line. Such a departure, I hereby attest, can result in powerful peer pressure, since the group's automatic reaction is to maintain its collective concepts, no matter how irrational these concepts may be in the light of reason. The relatively small minority of insignificant others, "heretics" in whose number I count myself, become expendable when they challenge the group.

I desire human love, support, and warmth; however, the fulfillment of these desires is not the prerequisite to my sobriety. Sobriety is my priority.

Ethically, I feel it is my daily responsibility to stay sober because I believe that I no longer have the right to chemically induced altered states. In the process of destroying my own life I endangered the lives of other human beings through my behavior while under the influence.

To accept the concept of utilizing a substitute addiction— reliance upon a mystical power greater than oneself—put forth in the programs of Alcoholics Anonymous and other support groups for alcoholism and drug addiction is, at worst, to involve oneself in an oppressive cultist atmosphere. At best, it is to encourage dependence upon something or someone other than oneself for sobriety, rendering sobriety conditional.

I maintain that, at this point in human history, due to humankind's collective scientific knowledge and acquired consciousness in the rational naturalistic sense, reliance upon a mystical source outside oneself can be a dangerous proposition, especially for the alcoholic.

A.A., you maintain that the sober alcoholic past the stage of physical withdrawal will, at certain times, have ". . . no effective mental defense against the first drink . . . ," that ". . . neither

he nor any other human being can provide such a defense . . . ,"
and, moreover, that ". . . his defense must come from a 'Higher
Power.' " I submit that this is an illusion.

I further submit that by printing this statement in your Big
Book, you give members at large license to be mean-spirited and
to reject those who will not or cannot conform. You know as
well as I that when newcomers walk out the door of an A.A.
meeting hall they are quite probably walking to their deaths, since
there is usually no alternative support group. I was one who walked
out after seven months of staying sober, several years prior to
my sobriety date. When I eventually returned to A.A., after my
first twenty-four hours free from alcohol, I was ready to accept
anything A.A. had to dish out.

I did not challenge the group my second time around. In
time, staying sober, I grew stronger, inspired by free-thought
literature—rather than by religion's milky mentality—securing a
firmer footing in my personal secular-humanist philosophies. No
god struck me down. I did not have to drink. Of course I must
maintain my sobriety daily, lifelong; this is *my* responsibility, *my*
challenge, *my* life.

As long as I stay sober, I will never again have to experience
the "call of the cells" or "required drinking" through the
resurrection of my physiological addition. One drink would trigger
my addiction and reactivate my all-consuming affliction, plunging
me into the abyss of alcoholism.

At this time in my life, I consider myself to be an agnostic,
naturalist, rationalist, skeptic, moderate existentialist, secular
humanist, and free thinker, among other things. I find no evidence
for God or a supernatural higher power in our natural universe;
I certainly don't know all the answers; no one does. And, although
life has no meaning per se, it is up to me to pump meaning
into it on a daily basis.

When, at times, it seems I have little going for me due to
life's problems—problems with friends, loss of a job, illness, anxiety,
fear, anger, guilt, etc.—*I still have my sobriety*. I don't always have

to like myself or every situation or to experience life as a mindless, all-goes-well television show; my sobriety is not conditional. I am the guardian of my sobriety in the here and now; it never goes on automatic pilot. Placing my personal sobriety above all else, acknowledging daily that I am an alcoholic, and working out from that point, I maintain awareness and acceptance of my disease.

Gods or goblins have nothing whatever to do with alcoholism, cancer, or any other disease. Agnostics, atheists, deists, secular humanists, and rationalists can achieve sobriety and maintain it *without* belief in the intervention of a higher power or "personal God."

We humans have a long history of stooping to fear and guilt tactics, intimidating and blaming the victim. This pathetic legacy fits neatly into A.A. meetings worldwide. It is obviously anti-free-thought and echoes the damage religious superstition has caused since the dawn of humankind, when man first shook a stick at the moon, partly rejecting and partly accepting his newfound capacity for rational thought.

"Frontal lobe blues"—not wanting to be aware of the human condition in a rational way or to act positively in light of the growing body of human knowledge in day-to-day life—are what religion and superstition are all about. Unfortunately, many more persons opt for these than for what truly makes us human: our ability to reason, to whatever degree we are individually and collectively capable.

Protecting this aforementioned "humanness" is how I stay alive, maintaining my personal sobriety *no matter what.*

Support groups are wonderful when they offer support without dogma; with dogma they are simply cults, casting out the non-believers.

Clearly, life and death are the issues here, nothing less. Alcoholics should not be coerced into giving up their individual identities and free-thought processes in order to be welcomed by so-called support groups, including Alcoholics Anonymous.

3 Why Stress Sobriety Over Alcoholism?

Alcoholism is the disease that I have. Sometimes I wish I could trade it in on a new model—athlete's foot, for instance. But it simply isn't possible.

Prioritizing sobriety makes living with alcoholism under "house arrest" most hopeful. Sobriety is my most precious asset, to be cherished and acknowledged daily, not to be taken for granted. It is not automatic like its dreadful counterpart, alcoholism. Sobriety is mine as long as I choose it daily above all else. I surrender to it fully, acknowledging my absolute need for it. And I have day after day of life, thanks to my willingness to choose sobriety, which imprisons my addiction to alcohol and allows me yet another twenty-four hours to work, play, and sleep in freedom and safety.

Not a bad deal, sobriety.

4 Me, Responsible?

Alcoholism research continues, judgmentalism lives, and the debate rages on as to whether the alcoholic is "responsible" for his or her alcoholism. Personally, I feel that the state-of-the-art research, pulling itself free from religion's influence, shows clearly enough that we do not bring about our own alcoholism. However, there can be no denying the obvious fact that each alcoholic must be responsible, at least after the initial withdrawal period, for maintaining his own sobriety. No god will save us, no one else can keep us sober. We are responsible for our sobriety on an individual basis.

Perhaps some people don't want to hear this. That is too damned bad.

We alcoholics inhabit a world full of living, breathing human beings. And some of them are MADD. Mothers Against Drunk Driving (and others) are fed up and their efforts have brought about important changes in our laws. Drinking alcoholics can ruin more than just their own lives. Alcoholics who claim, "I'm only harming myself," or, "It's my right, I never drive when I'm drinking," cannot see the sometimes subtle destruction they have wrought in the lives of others through their active addition to alcohol.

This is certainly not skirting the issue of irresponsible behavior of non-alcoholics who are under the influence. A car crash is a car crash. But obviously the odds for disaster are increased by chronic alcoholism—think about this instead of bemoaning the loss of a chilled martini.

5 Phasing Out the Pavlovian Pull

The Nobel-Prize winning Russian physiologist Ivan Petrovich Pavlov died in 1936, one year after the birth of A.A. Pavlov proved his theory of the conditioned response as a basic model of mental activity by regularly ringing a bell while feeding his dogs. He found that eventually the sound of the bell alone, even in the absence of food, caused the dogs to salivate; the dogs had become conditioned to associate the sound of the bell with food.

We alcoholics are also conditioned, especially in early sobriety and often even after years without alcohol. We chronically wish to repeat our drinking behaviors whenever we are reminded of drinking. I offer a reconstruction of the thoughts I had one typical morning early in my sobriety:

"Well, I think I'll (drink) brush my teeth and (drink) take a shower. After all, it's (drink) ten 'til eight and I'm (drink) due at the office by nine." The faint sound of a (drink) baby's cry is heard from an adjoining apartment. The phone rings (drink). I ignore it, thinking that answering might (drink) slow me down in getting ready for (drink) work. Flipping through the newspaper, I spot several (drink) liquor ads and (drink drink drink) open my refrigerator, noticing what looks like a booze bottle. Luckily, it is soda (drink).

The radio goes to a commercial break (drink) as I shave hurriedly.

The announcer enthusiastically tells of an extension of (drrinkk drink) "happy hour" at a local bar. Making sure my (drink) tie is on straight, I double check the front-door dead bolt. "Oh hi, Jim!" (drink d-d-r-r-r-i-i-n-n-k-k) my landlady sings out to me, as I attempt a smile and rush down the (drink) stairs.

And I never really drank in the morning.

You can imagine the balance of my newly sober day till I hit the pillow that night, having called another sober alcoholic during my lunch break, and having attended an A.A. meeting that evening, listening to "God talk" but being grateful for my sobriety.

How did I do it? I simply interjected secular mantras after each thought of drinking: "My name is _____ and I'm an alcoholic. I don't drink, *no matter what*," "Hello! I'm _____ . I'm an alcohol addict, I must not drink, I will not drink, no matter how I feel or what may happen to me today," "If I have to go crazy, I will do it sober."

Needless to say, these early days of sobriety are *crucial*. But eventually the Pavlovian pull weakens, one day at a time. As we newly sober alcoholics experience non-drinking behaviors—dealing with emotions, working, relating to others, replacing leisure-time drinking "skills" with sober coping mechanisms—all while prioritizing sobriety, we create new responses, desensitizing ourselves to the pull. We replace our addiction with our commitment to sobriety.

Systematic desensitization is achieved by "doing it sober." *It* is *everything*—aside from consuming alcohol. We've been consumed by alcoholism. We can replace this deadly consumption with sober experiences. Isn't it great, really, when you get right down to it, to know what's going on within us and with those around us. But even when it's not so great, we have at least learned, from the agony and our addiction, that sobriety is the answer.

6 Sobriety Strategies for the Newly Sober

You must first accept the fact that you are an alcoholic; that is, you are addicted to the drug and lose control if you ingest it. One or two drinks is never enough. If you've been through considerable pain and turmoil, if your denial mechanism is wearing down, if your health is virtually nonexistent, you're probably ready for what I call rag doll sobriety.

Rag doll sobriety is when one has been through the mill and is at long last ready for something—anything but more of the same. The fun has flown, drinking is more than a drag: the pain actually outweighs the need.

Your physiological addiction is killing you. You never planned it this way, you originally only wanted to enjoy a few drinks like everyone else. But physiologically, you are in fact not like everyone else—you're in the ten-percent league, a full-blown alcoholic. And you have a lot of company.

Welcome to sobriety. You are vulnerable, ready for any hope of an end to this nightmare you call your life (actually it's become a sub-life).

You hobble to your first A.A. meeting. You may be ready to accept anything, since you may rightly feel that everything you've tried to battle with has failed. Your conscious will and rationality are powerless in the face of chemical addiction at the cellular level.

That does not, however, mean that just because those smiling, sober A.A. faces, eyes sparkling (or glazed) with religion, hold the only key to your staying sober.

Or you may be a stubborn soul who, if the truth be known, is really only paying lip service to rationality. Your physiological need may be overpowering—you may be trapped within your cellular craving. The Pavlovian pull of your conditioned responses may be waiting to greet you, etched in your brain, as soon as detox time is over.

What then? Must you endure the ravings of religionists? Perhaps. Biding your time, you can take advantage of being around other sober alcoholics at A.A. or similar meetings. This is *not* to say you're better than the are; you're not. You're simply a nonbeliever. Be combative or feisty at your peril. They, my newly sober friend, are ready for you. This giant friendship machine has heard it all and they, like all theists, have answers for all your questions— usually answers like, "Shut up and listen," "Your 'best thinking' got you here," or "God will disclose more to us in His good time." Yes, it's possible to simply keep your mouth shut and celebrate sobriety.

But, fellow heretic, here's what you can do after each A.A. meeting: You can go home and devour free-thought literature, re- asserting your right to be you. Hopefully you won't reject sobriety, for if you do, you are a need personified—as they suspected. Hopefully you simply want to retain your identity, your rationality, your free- thought processes. You can, secretly if necessary, go to a local Unitarian minister, expressing your desire for secular support. If nothing comes of it, go to another one. Join various skeptical organiza- tions, read and reread free-thought literature. Know that you are not alone. Other nonbelievers, alcoholics sober many years, also inhabit this planet. Although throughout history the contributions of secularists equal those of mystics, many nonbelievers (as you well know) were tortured or executed, victims of whatever doctrine held reign at the time. Today, about all you have to contend with is peer pressure and annoying bumper stickers.

As you gain time in sobriety, prioritizing your sobriety above all else, acknowledging your sober alcoholic status daily, you'll find that the Pavlovian pull will weaken. Experiencing everyday life sober is new for you. You have the right to screw up, to fail, to lose, to feel miserable. Just don't drink. Trust the natural healing process.

Even in the most oppressive environment, you might in time want to start a Secular Sobriety Group. In the meanwhile, early on, place small inexpensive ads in all the free-thought publications you can get your hands on, noting that you're a recovering alcoholic agnostic or humanist or whatever label you feel comfortable with, and that you'd like to correspond with other sober alcoholic free thinkers.

This book offers some guidelines and suggestions to help you start a grass-roots group for nonreligious sober alcoholics. Remember, at this very moment, you are not alone. And you never have been alone—other sober alcoholic nontheists are out there. You have only to connect with them.

7 *No Matter What* Vignettes

In my first year of sobriety, a teenager stood trembling at an A.A. meeting. She said, "Hi. My name is Susan and I'm an alcoholic. And I don't drink *no matter what.*" That stuck with me. I took her declaration as my own.

After I first got sober, I saw my ex-lover being driven away in a new Lincoln. The new guy was rich, I was poor. But I had my sobriety.

I knew an elderly man who managed an apartment building in his retirement. He loved puttering around with potted plants while happily whistling along to recordings of organ music. He had been sober for thirty five years when he died of emphysema.

I encountered a fellow who, after some eight years of sobriety, was experiencing extremely hard times. So bleak was his situation that he was living in his car. I gave him what I could in the way of financial help, noting that nature in its random selection hadn't been terribly kind to the guy. He was quite disfigured. He was, however, quite sober.

There once was a fellow who, during his sobriety, lost three of his loved ones to suicide on separate occasions: his wife, his daughter, and his mother. He is still sober to this day.

I have seen AIDS patients who were also recovering alcoholics accept congratulations and acknowledgment for various periods of sobriety.

One man announced at a meeting that he'd set his hair on

fire if it were necessary to maintaining his sobriety. I believed him. He's still sober today.

To maintain sobriety—and thus to keep on living—we alcoholics must not reach for that bottle *no matter what*. Doing so can never help us; it can only plunge us into the depths of despair.

8 Little Things Mean A Lot

I remember one of the first movies I saw in my early sobriety. It was *The Buddy Holly Story*. This film was warm and moving, but my reaction to the very simple pleasure of seeing a good movie and living sober at the same time swept over me in the form of powerful feelings. I cried openly.

When I was drinking, I sometimes carried a concealed pint of vodka into the men's room of the theater, poured half my soda into the toilet, added vodka, stirred the contents hurriedly with my finger, and took a couple large gulps to keep me going. When I entered the theater lobby, already feeling the effects of the alcohol, I couldn't comprehend how pathetic my life had become—I had been such a movie buff, and now I couldn't even sit through a film without booze.

So seeing a movie sober was pretty damned special to me at the time.

9 Drink Dreams

I was walking from room to room upstairs in the glass house. A small dog and two bohemian types—male and female—were seated on the floor next to one of the many gigantic windows. All glass and wood. People singing. People arguing. Children running up and down the glass-and-wood stairs. Beautiful gleaming decanters of booze were available to all. I drank. Horrified, some friends looked my way, then pretended not to have seen. I was somehow drinking moderately. No addiction. Jesus! I was drinking!! But what had I done? This couldn't be happening to me. Funhouse laughter grew louder. I sweated and screamed out my pain, my guilt, my shame. This was the end: My beautiful sobriety had vanished. Wham!

I woke up and realized that it was only a dream. In reality I was still sober.

This and other dreams—the specifics of many, I can't vividly recall—have come to me over the years during my sobriety. They are horrifying—but what relief I feel when I awake! What joy, what peace of mind, what exhilaration!

Episodic "drink dreams" are common to most sober alcoholics. I have no problem with these dreams. In my early sobriety they came to me in clusters. The characters and locale change. A loneliness pervades some of these dreams. These days, after a number of years in sobriety, the dreams are less frequent. I have actually come to like their exotic tone. They, like all my dreams, are entertaining—

far better than most films I've seen recently. Maybe we "go crazy" in dreams, while warm and safe in our beds.

I would suggest that sober alcoholics enjoy these dreams, because the punch line is, *we're sober* when we wake up. And we can appreciate that passionately. We have our sobriety with which to face the day before us.

10 Spotlighting Sobriety for Survival

I heard that long ago someone asked, "How does A.A. work?" I understand the reply was, "Very well, thank you." This may elicit a chuckle, but when life and death are the stakes, understanding the process of recovery is vital.

There's nothing wrong with healthy skepticism—not to be confused with burned-out cynicism. Not knowing, at least generally, what makes something work *can* be dangerous. Why? During a crisis, one's life may be at stake—and with alcoholism that danger lurks, poised to strike at any moment. One cannot intuitively know what to hold onto in those moments of crisis.

I am convinced that the most important thing in all cases of long term, *no-matter-what* sobriety, is making sobriety one's first priority. The following are some examples of situations in which "Very well, thank you" might not suffice.

Tod, a secular humanist, had achieved several years of sobriety. He was doing okay—rather well, actually. His finances were on the upswing, as was his life in general. But he had become cocky about his sobriety and his alcoholism. He really didn't give it much thought anymore. It was good, feeling good, and he "couldn't be bothered." As he sat comfortably on a friend's yacht, transacting one of many successful business deals, he casually accepted a chilled

Mai Tai that his nonalcoholic host innocently offered him.

Weeks later, in another part of the country, broke and beaten down by his reactivated addiction to alcohol, he found himself reclimbing sobriety's ladder. Shaky and fearful, he was grateful to be alive.

John, a carpenter with a thirty-year drinking history and a strong personal religious belief, had achieved many months of hard-won sobriety. He was losing weight, doing well with romance and getting all the work he could handle. He was a loner and as a newly sober alcoholic he phased out his connection with other sober alcoholics, as well with his "bothersome" sobriety priority. One hot afternoon he walked into his favorite bar and ordered a double.

Joan, an articulate, intelligent, classy nontheist, had had a few years of sobriety. However, she had placed alcoholism about third on her list of priorities. Then a personal crisis jolted her into rearranging her life. She considers herself "very lucky" that she had no alcohol in her home at that crisis point. She remembered in the nick of time and did not drink.

George, an "A.A. golden boy," had been sober a number of years. As they say, he "worked a great program." He spread the word as an A.A. circuit speaker, traveling around the country. Caught up in A.A. activities, he had lost sight of an alcoholic's *key* to continuous living—*no matter what.* He had conditionalized his sobriety on some things that he wanted in his life. "God chose" not to give him those things and he drank. He is now deceased.

Of course life isn't fair. I'm sure at times we alcoholics would rather not be bothered with who we really are. So would cancer victims, diabetics, heart patients, and many others.

Life on life's terms is not always pretty. As sober alcoholics we must learn to cultivate new coping strategies, since we cannot cope courtesy of chemicals. We can still take breaks, nonchemical escapes. We can relearn fun in sobriety. Our lives as sober alcoholics can be filled with productivity, romance, and jolly good times as we trade addiction for commitment to sobriety.

11 The Sobriety Priority at Close Range

I have two "programs" in my life as a sober alcoholic:
1. My sobriety priority
2. Everything else

My sobriety priority is an issue separate from all else. Drinking is no longer an option in my life. As we live day by day, many of our actions become automatic and need not be considered daily. We can try to stick to our plans, schedules, diets, and commitments, but sometimes we screw up. It happens. Humans are imperfect. We pick ourselves up and go on.

As a sober alcoholic I must daily recommit, reaffirm, reaccept, resurrender, and reacknowledge my disease and its antidote: the sobriety priority. My priority frees me up for another day of life with all its pain, sorrow, joy, fear, sickness, achievements, failures, and goals, rather than trapping me in my previous sub-human, coma-like addiction to alcohol. Sobriety is assured *only* by prioritizing it daily on a day-at-a-time basis. This keeps my addiction to alcohol under "house arrest" day to day, hopefully lifelong.

I have the right to fail in any other area of my life. My sobriety priority is the one exception. As long as I reassert my priority every day, *no matter what*, I get to keep living, experiencing my personal adventure in a state of full awareness.

"Quality" of sobriety is spoken of by some as being important;

that is, "white knuckle" or "struggle sobriety" is considered inferior to relaxed sobriety. Actually, *all* sobriety is valid and is the same color and texture. Phases come and go. Tensions come and go. As long as sobriety is maintained, it is valid. All sobriety should be celebrated. Naturally we want to lead comfortable, relaxed, productive lives, to experience less pain and more pleasure.

Our best-laid plans can go awry but as long as our sobriety priority remains in place daily, the years pile up, culminating in a lifetime of sobriety. The quality of life lived during these sober years is up to the individual's limitations, efforts, and circumstances. Again, sobriety as one's priority must be a separate issue. How one's life unfolds has nothing at all to do with one's sobriety priority.

12 The Sobriety Priority and Conscious Choice

The sobriety priority is a way of life. For the alcoholic addict, abstinence from alcohol and all other mind-altering drugs is achieved through conscious choice. The choice process is not automatic. This choice is reaffirmed daily. Addiction to alcohol takes on a life of its own. One's sobriety priority never becomes second nature; it requires daily nurture.

The truth of it is, alcohol addicts must live their sobriety priority in twenty-four-hour segments in order to avoid (hopefully for a lifetime) a relapse. Reingesting alcohol or chemicals triggers the physiological addiction and reawakens associated behaviors and related feelings as well. Also, the reactivated physiological addiction grows worse as one ages. The longed-for moment of peace cannot be achieved by the alcoholic through drugs without a far steeper price of admission: loss, pain, torture, death.

Why would an addict put himself through all this? Scientists have found that when activated, chemical addiction is stronger than the sex drive. It reaches right into our primitive selves. Cellular addiction has no reason. It "knows" only its need.

Cellular addiction puts our newer, human equipment—frontal lobe reasoning and rational thinking—on hold. The same thing happens to nonaddicts when they drink. They can stop, not because of their reasoning powers, but because of their physiological differences. Thanks to their chemistry, not character, they can't tolerate any more. Willpower, intent, rationality, and inhibitions are immaterial. The alcoholic is always the loser.

Therefore to pretend that active alcoholism, once acknowledged, is something I used to do, not relevant to my new way of thinking and behaving, a fading memory, something polite society needn't discuss, best kept to myself, etc., to "let go and let God" can prove lethal.

The way for an alcoholic to stay sober is to acknowledge, every day, that he or she is an alcoholic who cannot, will not, and does not drink *no matter what*. Then and only then comes everything else: lover, family, friends, jobs, goals. One cannot mess around with cellular addiction. When one has a history of alcoholism, one must be willing, when necessary, to let everything else "go to hell" in order to stay sober.

Now, as you're well aware, daily life is usually not this colorful or dramatic. But the consequences of reactivated alcoholism are. Therefore, in this context, glib is out.

13 The Importance of Self-Reliance and the Danger of Superstition

Protecting our rational minds against wishful thinking defeats the denial process in alcoholism. Impaired judgment, whether induced by drugs or a religious or superstitious avoidance of reality, not only stunts an alcoholic's emotional growth, it puts him or her in real danger of drinking again.

The potential danger of superstition was brought home to me recently in my own life. I have several coffee mugs with drawings of cats on them. One of my mugs is black, with a beautiful black cat embossed on the side. I've used all of my mugs from time to time and have no particular favorite. A couple weeks back, while working on a project that I considered very important, I reached into the cabinet for a coffee mug and, though my hand came first to the handle of my black cat mug, I chose a yellow cat mug instead. I was rather absorbed in my work and thought little of my superstitious action. After all, hadn't I desensitized myself as a child by purposely walking into dark rooms, facing and dealing with my fear of the unknown? Hadn't I ignored foolish superstitions as far back as I could recall, walking under ladders, crossing the paths of black cats, telling friends who asked my "sign" that I put no stock in astrology?

Nonetheless, the next morning found me avoiding my black cat mug once again. I told myself, "This is silly. It's crazy. I'm giving this importance. Obviously the mug has no magical powers."

Then I thought, "But I'm working on a very important project right now. What if, on some level of consciousness, I place some importance, however small, in this and experience a self-fulfilling prophecy? What if I cause myself to somehow sabotage my work? The mind is a funny thing sometimes. Better to be safe and leave this alone, at least until my project is completed."

A few days passed and each day I would continue to avoid THE MUG. Then I caught a cold and was forced to stop working for a few days. During this interim period, when it came time to reach for a coffee mug once again, I reasoned that I'd better stop this nonsense now and poured the black cat mug full of coffee, feeling simultaneously relieved and freed. I had challenged the irrational fear and let's-play-it safe stance that had begun to flourish when I chose not to nip it in the bud. And by continuing to go out of my way to use the black cat mug beyond coffee—yes, even for drinking milk and water—I pulled this aberration out by the roots. Or did I? One cannot take for granted one's rationality and ability to reason. These abilities require nurture and exercise, which keep one's skepticism healthy and active.

Let us not kid ourselves. What the secular humanist philosopher Paul Kurtz refers to as the transcendental temptation[1] is every human's evolutionary gift at birth. It's up to us as individuals to exercise reason over fantasy. It is the daily choice of alcoholics to prevent a denial-relapse; therefore, swimming around in superstitious waters is not wise. Choosing the safer waters of the clear pool of reason allows me to swim sober.

Turning over one's sobriety and therefore one's life to something "greater" than oneself can be potentially hazardous to the health of a sober alcoholic. There are a lot of "powers" greater than myself. So what? A grizzly bear or a large dog or a deranged despot could make short order of yours truly. This has no bearing on my choosing sobriety. Muddled judgment is muddled judgment whether the muddling is brought on by booze, pills or religious superstition.

I suspect that everyone maintaining long-term sobriety practices the sobriety priority, whether or not he calls it by that name. And I suspect that at least a part of maintaining sobriety is self-protection through self-reliance, the avoidance of the dominance of one's natural "transcendental temptation," and the choice of reason over religious superstition.

14 Gullibility and the Grateful Syndrome

According to the *Random House Dictionary of the English Language,* to be grateful is to be "warmly or deeply appreciative of kindness or benefits received; thankful." Everyone feels grateful at various times.

Upon reentering life in a newly sober state, the nondrinking alcoholic is in a most vulnerable—almost infantile—position of helplessness. The alcoholic who has achieved sobriety after years of active alcoholism may well receive mixed messages. After all— disease or no disease—loved ones, friends, business associates, and others have had to experience the alcoholic's behavior, possibly for years. Perhaps the significant others in the alcoholic's life long ago bid him adieu, lovingly or otherwise. Perhaps he still has the support of family and friends.

Amends most typically are in order to those who have been the innocent victims of one's alcohol-induced behaviors. The research evidence is overwhelming: no one ever intended to become an alcoholic. Yes, many people, alcoholics and nonalcoholics alike, have intentionally abused alcohol and other drugs. They have, on certain occasions, intended to drink or to use drugs with abandon, regardless of the consequences resulting from their choice. Apparently, however, no one ever thought he would eventually become hooked. "It won't happen to me, I can handle it."

Countless others intended to drink responsibly and moderately, never dreaming they would experience problems with alcohol. But in time, as alcoholics, they too become enslaved by the drug.

When an alcoholic begins living sober, there is usually not a clean slate before him. The slate has at least some spots upon it—more often than not, dark blotches, mingled perhaps with human blood, certainly with human anguish. To the most compassionate, the most long-suffering among us, there are cut-off points. Society sees a bloody corpse mangled needlessly in a twist of car metal, an abandoned or brutalized child crying it's lungs dry in the night, a crucial commitment broken that leaves others innocently facing financial ruin. And society wants justice.

Society includes all of us, alcoholics too. It's often tricky to strike a balance between justice and mercy.

Freshly sober, detoxed and scared, feeling guilt and shame, the alcoholic begins his journey as a nondrinker. An alcoholic's primary objective must be the sobriety priority or we're right back where we started and we all lose. Does this mean that society should coddle the alcoholic? *No.* Through research, education, and treatment—not gods and faith healing—society can address this problem and should speak most firmly to the newly sober alcoholic regarding the responsibility to stay sober. This is a secular problem which requires a secular solution. The laying on of hands is no more effective here than it is in restoring a severed limb. Prayers may make some people feel good, but feeling good is certainly not the solution. An alcoholic should be told the truth as we know it, as it develops, rationally and scientifically.

Secular society can continue to roll up its sleeves and plunge its hands into the heart of the matter. We can deal with feelings rationally too, wiping the slate clean of religiously rooted judgmentalism. As for newly sober alcoholics, with or without those who offer them good wishes and support, they begin their new lives, make their amends (when and where appropriate) and pay their dues. Can they not do this with at least a touch of dignity?

Of course alcoholics are grateful to those who have suffered on their account, those who have loved and reached out to them.

How long into sobriety must an alcoholic crawl after attending to the wreckage of the past? Do guilt and shame on an ongoing basis breed responsibility? Isn't self-flagellation best left to medieval monks? Whether "character defects" played a part in one's alcoholism is irrelevant. If one is now sober and staying sober one need not pay heed to religious or secular priests—the purveyors of a how-we-should-feel, what-we-should-think, how-we-should-behave mentality.

Another definition of "grateful" from the same dictionary is "pleasing to the mind or senses; agreeable or welcome; refreshing."

Fortunate is another good word. I feel very fortunate to be sober today, to have a sober life, one day at a time; to have my life before me and, in sobriety, to have the option of choice. Yes, I'm grateful to those who put up with me in my active alcoholic state. I lucked out. I am fortunate that no one died beneath the wheel of a three-thousand-pound machine that I drove while under the influence on numerous occasions. And I did my best to make my amends. In sobriety I see more clearly who I really am. I don't always like what I see. I try to change negative characteristics and grow, but my ability to change and grow has nothing to do with my separate priority of staying sober.

Gullibility is pathetic at any stage of the game and I've been duped on occasion like most folks. One is especially susceptible in early sobriety. Gurus come out of the woodwork, exploiting one's vulnerability and gullibility. There is not a damned thing wrong with a newly sober alcoholic keeping an eye out for his own best interests. Yes, we're sorry. Now let's get on with it. And that goes for families, friends and associates. This is my new life, Charlie. Keep your spiritual guidance to yourself and wear it in good health. Let's try to work together in restructuring our relationships. Although no man is an island, no man need be a doormat. That was then, this is now. You can pray for me all you want, just don't prey on me.

Healthy skepticism flows through my veins in sobriety. It is ours for the taking. We were born with the grey matter that produces it. Choosing to use only the "feeling" portion of our genetic gifts is not only limiting, but downright dangerous for sober alcoholics. We do best to work our reason muscles and to keep them in tone, guarding against vulnerability and gullibility. Not only do we develop the good sense to refuse a drink, making alcohol a non-option, we also check things out a little more carefully in our sobriety. We now have the option to look before we leap, to think before we commit.

As with the sobriety priority, healthy skepticism and rational thinking never go on automatic pilot. We make our choices each and every day. We are wise to steer clear of quick-fix artists, in or out of clerical collars. Magical thinking often results from the "frontal lobe blues," but flexibility, acceptance, and a bit of daring are exhilarating in the sober lifestyle. If we feel our self-esteem growing day by day because we are staying sober, we become less vulnerable, less gullible, playfully feisty. Skeptical thinking frees us from the clutches of the grateful syndrome and from those relatives, friends, associates, and gurus who, in our previously drugged state, made mincemeat of our hearts and minds.

Brisk walks are great for building self confidence, altering one's state of consciousness and bringing about a feeling of well being. I'm grateful for good walks and moderate exercise.

Why not take a brisk sober walk to the registrar's office of a local community college and sign up for that course you always wanted to take? Perhaps you could lend your efforts in getting a better politician into office. You've seen enough corruption in the local school system; roll up your sleeves in glorious sobriety and proceed accordingly. Be a part of progressive change.

You're sober now. You're living responsibly. You've a right to participate and be heard. With skepticism and rationality comes activism. It's a natural surge of sober events. Take full advantage of your sobriety. You needn't cower in the corner. Work to bring about more secular approaches in educating others about alcoholism. An aware skeptic is less apt to be duped or enslaved. Start or join a local skeptics group or rationalists club. Remember also that many alcoholics, although sober, are products of the superstitious rather than the secular side of society. We have not only to "keep asleep" our addictions, we have unwarranted guilt and shame that religious teachings imprint in our brains as well. These messages of worthlessness can be challenged and overcome through logic, skepticism and positive activism. As we are no longer trapped in alcoholic blackouts, our reasoning minds are freed up. It is, however, up to us to use them. Not only are we the guardians of our sobriety, we are indeed the guardians of our thoughts, feelings and actions. Although we know we'll do a pratfall from time to time, we cannot drink. The point is that our quality of life sings inside us now. We can do anything that life demands and we can do it sober, undrugged, and unfettered by brain-damaging dogmas. We can be grateful without being gullible, and that's fortunate.

15 Secular Treatment for Chemical Dependency

We addicts are all in the same boat. Researchers now generally agree that chemical addiction is a real disease rather than "moral bankruptcy" and that a person suffering from an addiction to alcohol, cocaine, heroin, or another mind-altering drug is indeed subject to cross-dependency on other chemical substances.

Some researchers refer to alcoholism as ethanosis, that is, addiction to the narcotic ethanol (alcohol). Other researchers believe that a more accurate term would be acetaldehydism, since the body's oxidation of ethanol to acetaldehyde (a substance even more toxic than ethanol) results in higher acetaldehyde concentrations in the blood of alcoholics than in nonalcoholics who ingested the same amounts. And research points to complete abstinence as the only viable antidote for chemical addiction.

Researchers agree that character defects do not cause chemical addiction. Hospitals and clinics impart information to recovering addicts about how the body is harmed, and about the stages and development of cellular addiction; yet professionals at these institutions continue to shove A.A.'s twelve steps and "God as you understand Him" under the noses of cocaine addicts, alcoholics, heroin addicts, and all other chemical-dependent persons.

I recently visited a newly sober alcoholic in a local hospital alcoholism ward, and as the elevator door slid open, I was faced with a prominently displayed rack of religious A.A. literature. Though the hospital had no religious affiliation, I considered this to be about as secular as the entrance to a cathedral.

When I reached my friend's room, he expressed great relief at being able to talk, at last, to another free thinker. The therapists, he told me, had been working to help him find his Higher Power. Since he is a secular humanist, this didn't set too well with him; yet he wanted to live, he wanted to recover. He was sincere. He had a genuine desire to stay sober.

Nonreligious persons do not deserve this kind of response to their needs. Why can't we have secular chemical-dependency treatment in our supposedly secular hospitals and clinics?

Researchers give alcoholism professionals rational, scientific answers regarding drug addiction, yet these professionals continue to respond with prayers.

As stated earlier, sobriety is the only antidote to chemical addiction, and one must depend upon oneself, not religion, to achieve it. One does not achieve sobriety by ridding oneself of character defects. A chemically additive cellular need doesn't know a damned thing about character defects or morality. Nonreligious alternatives for sobriety maintenance should be available in our communities. There should be an option of truly secular treatment programs in our hospitals and clinics. We secular alcoholics also need places in which to share our stories, feelings, and sobriety strategies with one another.

Of course, both the religious and the nonreligious should try to be the best persons they can be. But some of the best persons are chemically addicted.

The focus for an addict should be on his or her priority of sobriety. All other values, goals, and principles must be reshuffled to fall in line behind sobriety. There are no short cuts. There are no viable alternatives. There is no easier way.

The sobriety priority could be the focus in treatment centers, and is the focus in grass-roots Secular Sobriety Groups.

We know so much more today than we did even ten years ago in regard to alcoholism and other chemical addictions. It is up to us now as a nation to act upon this body of knowledge, using what we know in secular centers for treatment and maintenance. Chemical addiction is a medically proven disease. It requires real medical treatment initially and nonsuperstitious rational adherence to the sobriety priority for the remainder of an addict's life.

16 A Secular Framework For Sobriety

Consider the following facts from the National Council on Alcoholism:

- Alcoholism is a chronic, progressive, and potentially fatal disease characterized by physical dependency or pathologic changes in the internal organs, or both.[1]
- Alcoholism and alcohol abuse occur in every socio-economic group, although the problems may manifest themselves differently in different groups.[2]
- Alcoholism is one of the most serious public health problems in the United States today. Among the 18.3 million adult "heavier drinkers" (those consuming more than 14 drinks a week), 12.1 million have one or more symptoms of alcoholism, an increase of 8.2 percent since 1980.[3]
- Alcohol is the most widely used—and abused—drug in America. In 1981, the equivalent of 2.77 gallons of absolute alcohol was sold per person over the age of 14. This equals about 591 12-ounce cans of beer, 115 fifths of table wine, or 35 fifths of 80-proof whisky, gin, or vodka. One-tenth of the drinking population consumes half the alcoholic beverages sold.[4]
- Alcohol abuse accounts for approximately 98,000 deaths annually, including those caused by cirrhosis and other medical consequences, and alcohol-related homicides, suicides, and motor-vehicle and other accidents.[5]

- $89.5 billion was the economic cost to the nation resulting from alcohol abuse and alcoholism in 1981. By 1983, the economic impact had reached $116.7 billion.[6]
- Alcoholism treatment reduces total health care costs. In a study of over 20 million claim records between 1980 and 1983, the families of alcoholics used health-care services and incurred costs at twice the rate of similar families with no known alcoholic members. On an average, the cost of the alcoholic's treatment was offset by reductions in other health-care costs within 2 to 3 years from the start of treatment.[7]
- Alcohol is known to cause or contribute to many fatal illnesses, including cardiac myopathy, hypertensive diseases, pneumonia, and several types of cancer.[8]
- One out of three American adults—56 million Americans— says that alcohol abuse has brought trouble to his or her family. This is about four times the number of families that say that other drugs have troubled their homes.[9]
- Chronic brain injury caused by alcohol is second only to Alzheimer's disease as a known cause of mental deterioration in adults. Mental deterioration through alcohol is not progressive; if the patient stops drinking, the deterioration is arrested and substantial recovery can occur.[10]
- Children of alcoholics have a four-times-greater risk of developing alcoholism than children of non-alcoholics. There are 28.6 million children of alcoholics in the U.S. today, 6.6 million of whom are under the age of 18.[11]
- Genetic influence can be identified in at least 35 percent to 40 percent of alcoholics and alcohol abusers, and it affects both men and women. People whose family history involves alcohol abuse face increased risk. Furthermore, many types of alcohol abuse may exist, each with its own genetic predisposition interacting with a particular environment.[12]
- An estimated 3.3 million drinking teenagers aged 14 to 17 are showing signs that they may develop serious alcohol-related problems.[13]

- Recent surveys conducted in the United States indicate that a person's first drinking experience usually occurs at around the age of 12, in contrast to age 13 or 14 in the 1940s and 1950s. It is no longer unusual for 10-to-12-year-olds to have serious alcohol abuse problems.[14]
- Since 1966, the number of high school students nationwide who get intoxicated at least once a month has more than doubled, from 10 percent to more than 20 percent.[15]
- Most youth begin to drink regularly during adolescence. A recent study found that alcohol is the most widely used drug among young people between the ages of 12 and 17.[16]
- About 30 percent of fourth-grade respondents to a 1983 *Weekly Reader* poll reported peer pressure to drink beer, wine, or liquor.[17]
- 11 percent of New York State public-school students in grades 7 through 12 described themselves as being "hooked" on alcohol.[18]
- By ninth grade, more than half (56 percent) of the high school seniors responding to a 1982 national survey had tried alcohol. By their senior year, more than 9 out of 10 had done so.[19]
- Fetal Alcohol Syndrome (FAS) is the third leading cause of birth defects and the only preventable one among the top three. The incidence of FAS is approximately 1 in 750 live births, or 4,800 babies a year. Thirty-six thousand newborns each year may be affected by a range of less severe alcohol-related fetal alcohol effects (FAE).[20]
- Women frequently engage in the high-risk practice of abusing other drugs in combination with alcohol. A 1983 Alcoholics Anonymous survey showed that 40 percent of female A.A. members reported addiction to another drug. The number increased to 64 percent for women 30 years and under.[21]
- In 1984 there were 44,241 highway deaths; 53 percent were alcohol-related.[22]
- About 65 out of every 100 persons in the United States will be in an alcohol-related car crash in their lifetime.[23]

- Alcohol-related highway deaths are the number-one killer of 15-to-24-year-olds.[24]
- Alcohol is a contributing factor in at least 15,000 fatal and six million nonfatal injuries in nonhighway settings.[25]
- Between 400 and 800 boating fatalities annually involve alcohol. Alcohol is implicated in 65 percent to 69 percent of all reported drownings.[26]
- Alcoholics are 10 times more likely to die from fires than nonalcoholics, 5 to 13 times more likely to die from falls, and commit suicide from 6 to 15 times more frequently than the general population.[27]
- Drinking is estimated to be involved in about 50 percent of spouse-abuse cases and up to 38 percent of child-abuse cases.[28]
- Fifty-four percent of prison inmates convicted of violent crimes were drinking before they committed the offense. Sixty-two percent of those convicted of assault had been drinking. Forty-nine percent of those convicted of murder or attempted murder had been drinking.[29]
- Between 2 and 10 percent of people 65 and over experience some type of alcohol-related problem. Approximately 25 percent of the age 65-plus population is on some form of medication. By most measures, older people consume more medication than any other age group, putting them at high risk for drug and alcohol interaction.[30]

It's not surprising that the A.A. philosophy, complete with its twelve steps and higher power, is used in secular settings. Hospital chemical dependency/alcoholism wards, large corporations, and courts of law utilize A.A. in its original format. This is so partially because A.A. has, for over fifty years, offered an effective approach for dealing with alcoholism.

Although its approach is clearly religious, it does bring results, despite its "spiritual" thrust. This is primarily because it offers a framework for breaking the cycle of denial and advocates an honest desire to stop drinking.

Dryout clinics existing prior to A.A. could *get* people sober, but offered no follow-up to *keep* them sober. For decades, the psychological community has researched the *why* of alcoholism. But in the last decade the concept of an alcoholic personality has been left by many to dry in the wind.

Perhaps part of the problem is that psychiatry and psychology are not hard sciences. A well-known gay activist told me about an event that took palce in 1973: Following years of extensive lobbying by gays, the American Psychiatric Association, after sending a referendum to its many members, voted (by 58%) to remove homosexuality from the books as a mental illness. What other science votes facts in or out of its texts? Are psychiatrists and psychologists secular priests? Is psychology sometimes an extension of theology, secularized?

It is physiologists who have come up with some rather impressive research regarding alcoholism. Perhaps hard science is humanity's elegant version of common sense in practice; postulates borne out by hard data. The scientific method moves us forward; religion and its derivatives detain us. And A.A. always had common sense at its core, shining forth despite its religiosity.

"Put the plug in the jug," say A.A. members. And keep away from the jug, because its contents, if you are addicted at the physiological level, will control your life. So how do you put the plug in the jug and keep it there? And what do you do about the previous alcoholic experiences now etched in your brain? How do you live happily with the jug plugged?

As a sober alcoholic who has experienced plugged-jug living, I offer the following suggestions as secular guidelines for achieving and maintaining sobriety. Some of these strategies were passed on to me by others, some I discovered by accident—but all have been vital to my plugged-jug lifestyle.

I am an alcoholic.

If you need to be convinced, have trouble with the word or concept, or cannot accept that you are an alcoholic, you're probably trapped, experiencing denial, and there's not a damned thing anyone can do for you at this point unless you take action by reaching out. As a sober alcoholic, I *urge* you to get help now. Contact your doctor or a local hospital and get an evaluation by alcoholism professionals.

I choose sobriety one day at a time.

I acknowledge that I am physiologically addicted to the drug, alcohol, and that my alcoholism has taken on a life of its own. I am ready to reclaim my life, to live one day at a time as a *sober* alcoholic. I accept that I cannot drink *no matter what*. As an alcohol addict, having experienced many years of problem drinking and having experienced loss of control in drinking, I choose to prioritize my sobriety one day at a time. I no longer deny my alcoholism, since it has become obvious to me. My sobriety priority is a separate issue for me. This simple strategy of placing my sobriety priority above all else allows me to reclaim my life and realize my full potential one day at a time.

I never intended to become physiologically hooked on alcohol. Alcoholics and nonalcoholics alike have used and abused alcohol. Moderate drinkers, heavy drinkers, those who drink to numb their feelings, to temporarily escape conflicts and anxieties, to celebrate or brighten an already pleasurable event, become hooked on the drug *if* they are physiologically unable to process it safely; that is, if they are alcoholics.

Having broken the cycle of denial, no longer allowing a physiological need to masquerade as me, I have the opportunity of choice available to me now.

My sobriety priority is the antidote to my alcoholism. My sobriety priority is not simply abstinence. It is my positive, conscious, rational choice to stay sober one day at a time.

As a sober alcoholic, I reach out to others.

As a sober alcoholic, I now have the opportunity to evaluate my situation, reaching out when appropriate to the others in my life who may have suffered directly or indirectly from my behavior when I was under the influence.

When did I begin drinking? When did my drinking begin to manifest itself as a problem? When did feedback from others begin regarding my drinking? Who were these people? Would it be appropriate to contact them and to inform them of my regrets, to apologize? Or would doing so cause them harm or problems? Am I relieving my own stored-up guilt at their expense? Do I owe something to someone, financially or otherwise? Are certain situations, in my judgment, best left alone? I can prepare lists, take notes, and make imperfect but sober decisions. What about my loved ones? Which of my relationships can be salvaged? It's up to me to find out in sobriety.

As a sober alcoholic, I experience myself in real ways.

One's undrugged feelings, thoughts, and personality can be experienced in sobriety. Probably no human being has ever been completely satisfied or comfortable on all occasions with who he perceives himself to be. We're imperfect. But we can work to change.

We learn to live with some of our "warts" and to accept them as part of who we are. We can make lists of our personal assets and liabilities, our negatives and positives as we perceive them, working for a blend of self-acceptance, change, and growth. *If* we maintain our sobriety priority, we always have, as sober addicts, a built-in self-esteem. But to keep that, we must choose sobriety as *number one* on our value and survival scale in daily life.

As a sober alcoholic, it is my responsibility to give my own life meaning.

Although life has no meaning per se, we can stay sober even through the "meaningless" segments, simply by prioritizing sobriety, *no matter what.* Plunging into life also nets us coping skills acquired in the process of living sober. Life is, for all organisms, an ongoing process. In doing and experiencing all things *sober*—no matter what our reactions to life's challenges are—we become more flexible. Uncertainties are a matter of course.

Accepting—not necessarily *liking*—life's uncertainties allows us to grow as persons. We learn. Answers and solutions develop for us. Discomfort is a part of life for all of us. Coping skills are developed by "doing it sober," as we accumulate one sober experience after another.

In early sobriety, sharing thoughts and feelings and going into the world with another sober alcoholic benefits both participants and eventually leads to solo sober excursions into the marketplace of experiences.

Make a list of situations in which you'd like to feel more comfortable. This will weaken your alcohol associations as you do more things without the crutch that alcohol can provide.

Anxiety is normal. In any given situation, a rush of a combination of feelings may occur. This will happen less with each experience. Take a sober alcoholic "buddy" or a nonalcoholic who is a trusted friend or professional with you on these desensitization excursions. If the other person does not live up to your expectations, temporarily abandon the project and do it later with another buddy.

In my early sobriety, I went with two of my sober alcoholic friends to a loud, lively, crowded disco bar and had a great time! We ordered soft drinks (preferably in the can or bottle, not poured, to avoid busy-bartender botch-ups) and really enjoyed the experience, while desensitizing ourselves to a situation we'd previously associated with booze.

Another shy newcomer and I purposely positioned ourselves at the entrance of a large work-related convention we were both obliged to attend. After saying, "Hello, hope you enjoy your evening" and handing out brochures to several thousand people, one becomes less anxious about crowded social situations.

These desensitization experiences can be entered into at your own pace. As A.A. might say, "Easy does it, but do it!" Experiencing by doing brings meaning into one's life. Sober meaning.

17 Living Well in Sobriety Is the Best Revenge

I've never met an addict who chose to become an addict. Some of us chose to be "party animals" and use mind-altering chemicals irresponsibly. Others were quite moderate and conscientious in their consumption of these chemicals. When addiction set in, for all of us, it was the equalizer.

In our sober lives we can and should be very good to ourselves. We can pursue our dreams, work toward our goals, partake in life's numerous drug-free pleasures and experiences. We feel better now than when we were younger and active in our addictions, why not look the part as well? Lose those surplus pounds. If your hairline is receding, why not get a transplant? Buy a new wardrobe. Work out in a gym. Travel. Start a new relationship. Reasonable hedonism has its place. Why not cherish these sober years and relish the sober times of our lives?

I visited the Grand Canyon in my drinking days and also saw Hawaii through the window of my hotel room while recovering from hangovers. My sober years are so much fuller for me, even in hard times. A walk in the park is lovely, and feeding the squirrels beats falling to my hands and knees, throwing up in some strange toilet bowl.

Enjoying a Sunday ride in the country rivals being laid up for days from an alcohol-related car accident. Why not try the things in sobriety that you postponed when you were chemically detained?

As you gain time in sobriety, you will find problems and challenges in day-to-day living, as does every other human being, alcoholic and nonalcoholic alike. And since drinking is no longer an option for you, your problems and challenges will no longer be simply with staying sober.

At times we will experience "white knuckle living"—not "white knuckle sobriety"—since sobriety is separate, a daily point of reference from which you proceed *no matter what*. Stress and anxiety plague us on occasion and it is, by and large, a myth that we can experience zombie-like serenity on an ongoing basis in real life. Don't feel bad! No one is perfect, that's not the nature of things. Glassy-eyed serenity can be found in religious cult groups, but the reality of life has a way of seeping into one's consciousness. We humans have this newer mental equipment, bequeathed by evolution, to contend with. We can't throw it off when we experience "frontal lobe blues." Magical thinking only goes so far and is, in the long run, potentially dangerous for an alcoholic.

So, pure serenity—feeling that all is well with the world on an ongoing basis—is, for most of the human race, elusive and inconsistent.

We all have imperfections. We all have troubles. Things often go smoothly but life circumstances can change. We can adapt to these changes. We don't always have to be thrilled with these changes or to pretend that we are serene "no matter what."

When drinking is no longer an option for us, the protected, separate issue of our sobriety priority allows us to go on with our day, come what may, doing our best. At times we don't do our best, don't really try to do much of anything. This has nothing whatsoever to do with our sobriety priority.

It hurts to try hard and still experience failures, losses, and injustices. We feel bad. We feel good. We feel anxiety. We feel strength, weakness, fear, and joy. These feelings have nothing at all to do with the prioritized separate daily issue of our sobriety.

Religions and movements that demand unthinking adherence also make false promises. One's environmentally protected bubble can burst. Hot air balloons are only temporary.

The sobriety priority makes no promises and guarantees nothing. How can it? It is simply a strategy, and construct, a technique that, when applied daily, frees us to live our lives, wherever they may lead us.

The sobriety priority is a crisp, honest concept, free from religion and false promises regarding reaching certain plateaus, levitating, avoiding taxes, or living forever in a disembodied aftermath, floating perhaps in and out of black holes.

No one has really ever escaped living life on life's terms, unless one considers living a comatose existence via drugs or religion or thoughtless adherence to a cause. Those of us who do not try to throw off our rational human mental equipment learn to appreciate, accept, yes, even run with life on life's terms. But certainly, we cannot pretend our primitive limbic systems, our cellular, needy, emotional selves are not equally important.

We've got all this going for us. Yes, it's complex. It's challenging. It's downright exciting, being a human being participating in this very real adventure of life.

That's right. The glass is half full, not half empty; but the sobriety priority doesn't demand any certain attitude toward a quality of life.

Actually, the sobriety priority can be activated by anyone choosing to stay sober one day at a time. What one does with life during sober days is obviously an individual choice, to the extent that one can make a choice regarding growth, action, and achievement, not using other human beings to measure oneself against. Other human beings are human beings, not yardsticks.

Do any of us really know if we're doing our best? Somewhat, but my best is not your best. So living and rising to some of life's challenges is generally thought to be the right course.

Each sober alcoholic is responsible for his own sobriety. Human support makes us feel good. No one can reach into our innards to keep us sober, although some people I've encountered have been so caring that they would have done so had it been humanly possible.

You have the right to do what you will with your sober time. And although what goes around does not necessarily come around, we all must pay the price for our choices.

Opting for a life of involvement, productive activity, reasonable risk-taking, and active participation in the adventure *is* an option for us.

The adventure of life for alcoholics in sobriety is multi-faceted. It is full of fun, challenges, and choices. Even when we fall on our faces (as I often do) we can choose to do it sober. No longer sleeping in one's own vomit (as I often did) can be refreshing in itself. Even experiencing pain and anxiety is at least ours; it's real, not chemically induced. We're alive! We leave the sub-human status of active alcoholism behind and progress daily in sobriety.

The first year in sobriety is best reserved for reentry, avoiding major decisions whenever possible, allowing time for mental cobwebs to clear away. Sobriety offers no guarantees of growth, fortune, or true love; but without sobriety, as alcoholics, we will never achieve any of these.

We can learn to laugh, cry, and feel again, to know who we are, to celebrate our sobriety in the recovery process. Self-actualization is now possible. So obey the laws of the land, beware the emptiness of the long-distance hedonist, be well, and enjoy!

As a sober alcoholic, you can now do the everyday things taken for granted by so many: shower, shave, wear clean clothing, wash your hair, brush your teeth, eat well, speak clearly, sleep soundly.

You will begin to feel better about yourself and more attractive to others if you take the time to pamper yourself. Buy new clothing; visit a beautician or barber; wear makeup, perfume, or aftershave; get a facial or massage; wear expensive or formal clothing occasionally; work on your suntan; join a health club; visit a sauna; get your teeth cleaned or fixed; buy new glasses; improve your diet.

You may find conversation difficult in your early days of sobriety, but the topics available are virtually limitless: sports, philosophy, your health, your children or grandchildren, sex, politics, current events, religion, people, your job or schoolwork. Don't be afraid to ask for advice or help, to argue, or to be assertive or stubborn. You may even begin to like talking to others so much that you will decide to take up public speaking or lecturing.

There are many activities and events you can enjoy sober. They include attending concerts, operas, ballets, plays, weddings, graduations, bar mitzvahs, social or civic club meetings, government meetings, court sessions, lectures, banquets, luncheons, school reunions, and alumni meetings. You can go to a fair, carnival, circus, amusement park, zoo, park, picnic, barbeque, museum, or exhibit, a movie or drive-in, and the library; attend auctions and garage sales; go shopping; just go downtown and mingle. Many events are free and you can learn while being entertained.

Be creative! At one time you may have been interested in pursuing the arts and have subsequently let your talents fall by the wayside. Or you have always wanted to try your hand at painting, drawing, sculpture, acting, movie-making, composing or arranging music, creative writing, singing, or playing a musical instrument. Now is the time!

Take up a sport: softball, baseball, basketball, football, boating, tennis, water-skiing, bowling, wrestling, boxing, fishing, horseback riding, badminton, shuffleboard, croquet, horseshoes, ping-pong, snowmobiling, swimming, running, jogging, gymnastics, aerobics, frisbee, catch, soccer, rugby, skiing, lacross, hockey, bicycling, handball, paddleball, squash, surfing, and scuba diving are just a few of the sports available. If you do not think you are physically capable of one of these, try cards, chess, checkers, board games, or party games; or just attend a sporting event. Cheering your team as a spectator is often as much fun as active participation.

If all the activity becomes too much for you, there are many ways to rediscover nature. Go for a ride in the country, a hike in the mountains, or a stroll on the beach; watch wild animals; listen to the sounds of nature; look at the stars, sky, clouds, or a storm; smell a flower; walk barefoot; go birdwatching, beachcombing, or mountain-climbing; gather natural objects such as rocks, driftwood, or wild food; take a field trip. If you live in a metropolitan area and cannot get away, become an "urban explorer": take a walk in the city and notice the unexpected oases of nature there; make a snowman; hang a bird-feeder in your backyard; buy an aquarium. Observing nature can be a peaceful experience in even the most crowded environments.

You will find that as a sober alcoholic, you have more spare time to spend on things you enjoy doing. Learn a new craft or skill; restore antiques; refinish furniture; take up woodworking or carpentry; hone your mechanical skills; learn a foreign language or American Sign Language; make food or crafts to sell or give away; invent something; take up gardening, landscaping, or yard work; learn photography; try your hand at writing articles, essays, reports or scholarly papers; become a gourmet cook; can, freeze, or preserve foods; rearrange or redecorate your room, house, or apartment; work with beads, leather, or fabrics; make pottery or jewelry; take up knitting, crocheting, sewing, or needlework; do a scientific experiment; repair something.

Spend time alone: write in a dairy; stay up late; meditate or do yoga; read the newspaper, stories, poems, novels, plays, "how-to-do-it" books or articles, essays, comic books, academic or professional literature, or magazines; people-watch; write letters, cards, and notes; care for houseplants; spend time with your pet; collect things; take a walk; sleep late or get up early; listen to music; visit a cemetery and remember a departed friend or relative; watch television; cry; do odd jobs around the house; enjoy the peace and quiet; think positively about the future; talk to yourself; solve a puzzle; think about someone you like; daydream; sing to yourself; listen to the radio; scream out your frustrations or anger; work on your finances; think about your problems.

Perhaps the most fulfilling thing a newly sober alcoholic can do is spend time with other people. This may be difficult at first, but going out of your way will be worth the effort. Make a new friend; travel in a group; become acquainted with a neighbor; visit old friends and reminisce; teach or coach someone; give a massage or backrub; do someone a favor; help with someone's problems; tell a joke to lift someone's spirits (and your own!); confess or apologize to someone you may have hurt; smile at people; express your love to someone; have tea, coffee, or soft drinks with friends; be with children; give or attend a party; go to a family reunion; have lunch or dinner with friends or associates; have a frank and open conversation; try to be outgoing at a gathering; go dancing; congratulate someone; go on a date; join an encounter or therapy group; enjoy physical contact with someone; introduce people to each other; give gifts, send letters, make telephone calls; buy something for someone; meet someone of the opposite sex; loan something; counsel someone; compliment someone; join a fraternity or sorority; play a harmless practical joke; tell someone you need him or her.

Once you have taken the first steps toward becoming more outgoing in your personal life, you may be comfortable branching out into the public sphere. You can do volunteer work; visit the sick, shut-ins, or people in trouble; work on a political campaign; protest something; join a neighborhood group; defend or protect someone; help stop fraud or abuse. Become more involved with your work: attend a business meeting, luncheon, or convention; give a speech or lecture; pay more attention to details; and when you are offered that raise or promotion, accept it with pride!

18 Conversation

"Well, I guess you've licked your alcohol problem." He was most sincere, a nonalcoholic sipping his coffee with us at a small table tucked in a cozy corner of the large restaurant. My other nonalcoholic friend lingered over her chocolate soda and asked, "What exactly is it you do to stay sober? I mean, is it a state of mind, or what? Now, if I'm probing too much, you know me well enough just to tell me to shut up. Right?"

It's not unusual for nonalcoholics to assume you've licked your alcohol problem if you have experienced a substantial period of continuous abstinence from alcohol. They believe that's that, so to speak. With the postscript, "of course you'll never drink again, now that this alcoholism thing is behind you."

"What exactly is it you do to stay sober? I mean is it a state of mind, or what?" My two friends were interested in a new Secular Sobriety Group I'd recently started for alcoholics uncomfortable with A.A. and other religious approaches to sobriety. I explained as best I could that our priority is staying sober and that we meet once a week in a friendly, informal, candlelit atmosphere to share our thoughts and feelings as alcoholics living sober.

"As you know," I said, "I've never kept my alcoholism a secret. I'm proud of my sobriety. Some other things in my life I'm not so pleased with, but sobriety is my most precious asset, my priority, my life-and-death necessity. When you choose to socialize with someone who has a physical disability—say, a person in a wheelchair—you accept the person for who he or she is, wheelchair and all. Some people prefer not to be bothered with a disabled friend. In my case, you know I don't drink, but you invite me anyway, offering a can of soda pop instead of a martini.

"Now, from a factual perspective, I am just as alcoholic as I was prior to achieving sobriety; that is, I must reaffirm daily my priority of staying sober *no matter what!* I go to the market, work, see movies, make love, eat, sleep—all as a sober alcoholic. I'm a person with an arrested but lifelong disease. I place my sobriety and the necessity of staying sober before anything else in my life. Those who have had a terrible experience go on with their lives but they have the *experience* etched into their psyches. It never goes away. Neither does my alcoholism; the etchings of my chronic alcoholism experience and my dormant physiological addiction wait to be awakened with that first drink. Alcoholism results in the inability to control one's drinking. Sobriety requires the acknowledgment of one's alcoholism on a daily basis, and it is never to be taken for granted. I must endure all my feelings and experiences, including injustices, failures, and whatever this uncertain life doles out. I can't drink, *no matter what* comes down the turnpike.

"So," I continued, "in answer to your questions: I have my alcohol problem licked only on a daily basis and I continue to stay alive by protecting my conscious mind, by staying sober and avoiding the muddy waters of religion. I can't deal with reality by way of fantasy.

"A.A. and other groups fight demons with dogma or gods or the 'powers' of belief and faith. That's too scary for me. The more I stay in reality, in rationality, the better my chances. So, yes, my sobriety is a state of mind rather than mindlessness."

The waitress refilled my coffee cup, and my friends and I shuffled small change and small talk about. In the parking lot we said our good-nights and headed for our cars. Mine needed a head gasket and was difficult to start; no amount of prayer, conjuring, or belief would improve its performance. So it is with the disease of alcoholism.

19 This Is Serious

I have a friend who has about four years of sobriety. He attends A.A. conventions regularly, and tells me that at these conventions when a show of hands is requested regarding length of sobriety, thousands of hands are raised acknowledging weeks, months, or even a couple years. But as the number of years called out climbs upwards of three years, only a smattering of hands is raised. This is not a statement about the effectiveness of A.A. per se, although that's a factor. Rather, it is a revelation of fact regarding alcoholism and the sobriety priority: Sobriety must be prioritized afresh daily; to do otherwise sooner or later allows sobriety to die.

If long-term, lifelong sobriety is not an alcoholic's goal in daily life, he or she will not prioritize sobriety.

I long for the day when convention halls filled with sober alcoholics will virtually burst at the seams, giving the local fire marshall concern from all the hands raised by all the long-term sober bodies, reflecting priority in action.

20 Secular Sobriety Groups: An Introduction

I believe that alcoholics are *all* allies in sobriety and our mutual goal is simply to achieve and maintain sobriety as individuals and to support one another, regardless of religious belief or unbelief. I, for one, cannot base my sobriety on things that go bump in the night.

Therefore, as a secular humanist, I suggest an alternative that opens the doors to *all* alcoholics, including us infidels, and patches the gaping holes in the safety net of A.A.: support meetings that are secular and do not require belief in a higher power.

We free thinkers simply want to have a life of sobriety, one day at a time. Since nontheists have no afterlife to look forward to, let's join hands in this life.

In Los Angeles, in November 1986, I convened a Secular Sobriety Group. We rely on rational intelligence and human emotions, and have shown by the success we've had so far that one need not be mystical to be merry, or go from grog to God in order to stay sober.

We've been meeting in a local parks-and-recreation facility one evening a week. Our gatherings there are informal. We have neither dues nor fees and ask only for small donations to help defray the costs of room rental and refreshments.

The Secular Sobriety Group (S.S.G.) has been publicized in a number of area newspapers and on local radio stations at no charge, because of our nonprofit, grass-roots status. The response has been most gratifying. We have been receiving an average of two telephone calls a day. The callers range from recovering alcoholics and their family members to humanist therapists inquiring on behalf of alcoholic clients, all in search of an alternative approach to A.A. and other religious alcohol-and-drug-addiction support groups.

Members range from the newly sober to those who have been sober for many years, and include carpenters, social workers, actors, office clerks, athletes, nurses, schoolteachers, and more. We are keeping the structure of our meetings loose and dogma-free. We simply stress the life-and-death necessity of alcoholics staying sober, and we encourage one another to cultivate an internal freedom from alcohol and other mind-altering drugs—*no matter what* happens in our lives that might contribute to a relapse.

I question the value of individual anonymity as espoused in many support groups. Sharing openly my awareness of what I have recovered from and what a relapse would do to me is a critical truth—not a shameful secret to be revealed only at closed meetings and discovered by others only by accident. Certainly, marching down Main Street with placards is not what I am advocating, but I have come to realize that my relative openness has been a important factor for personal growth, contributing to a more comfortable life.

Some of our members prefer anonymity; others offer their full names, telephone numbers, and even business cards.

Although we welcome *all* alcoholics to our meetings, our approach is especially attractive to nonreligious persons.

Lives are being saved and made fruitful. There are no gods or goblins at our meetings. No belief in a higher power or adherence to any party line is required for sobriety. Our bond is a human one, natural but not supernatural, and so is our health and success. We value free thought over mind control and over mindlessness. But most of all, we celebrate and support all alcoholics in achieving and maintaining sobriety, regardless of their belief or nonbelief.

21 The S.S.G. Alternative

The alcohol/chemical addiction problem in this country is statistically astronomical, and certainly it is tragic. Lives are being wasted all across the land. All sorts of people suffer from these addictions; their relatives, friends, and colleagues are battered emotionally and sometimes physically as well. This cannot be denied; it is our situation, here and now.

Over fifty years ago when two men (an ex-stockbroker and a medical doctor, both alcoholics) started what was to become Alcoholics Anonymous, they brought to light what previously had been shoved under the national rug. They openly acknowledged the problem, ending what had previously amounted to massive collective denial, and offered an answer, a real solution. And for that they deserve applause from all those affected, directly or indirectly, by alcoholism/addiction—applause to the point of bringing blood to the palms. And those affected include just about everyone in the United States and around the globe.

One of these men, Bill Wilson, was inspired by the then soon-to-be-defunct ultra-rigid religious organization called the Oxford Group. He had dropped his personal agnostic stance because of the sudden and powerful religious experience he had there, though he eventually broke away from the group.

Because in those days society viewed alcoholics as pariahs, Bill and "Dr. Bob" built A.A. on a first-name-only basis. The literature of A.A. reflects the widespread belief that the causes of alcoholism are character defects and an unknown factor. The theory was basically this: Put the plug in the jug, turn your will and your life over to the care of God as you understand Him, work on your character defects through A.A.'s twelve-step spiritual program, and carry the message to other alcoholics. Unlike the Oxford Group, members of A.A. did not strive for spiritual perfection. Instead, more realistic spiritual progress was their goal: "We are not saints," reads the Big Book of A.A.

Today, though its founders are deceased, Alcoholics Anonymous remains alive and well—fortunately. However, A.A. is religious (or "spiritual") requiring belief in a mythical higher power, which is a meaningless concept to many free thinkers. Let's face it folks, its founding fathers based the group on their beliefs and, although A.A. apologists try to get around it, A.A. remains a spiritual movement. And that's fine for spiritual people.

Here are the famous twelve steps of Alcoholics Anonymous:

1. We admitted we were powerless over alcohol—that our lives had become unmanageable.

2. Came to believe that a Power greater than ourselves could restore us to sanity.

3. Made a decision to turn our will and our lives over to the care of God as we understand Him.

4. Made a searching and fearless moral inventory of ourselves.

5. Admitted to God, to ourselves, and to another human being the exact nature of our wrongs.

6. Were entirely ready to have God remove all these defects of character.

7. Humbly asked Him to remove our shortcomings.

8. Made a list of all persons we had harmed, and became willing to make amends to them all.

9. Made direct amends to such people wherever possible, except when to do so would injure them or others.

10. Continued to take personal inventory and when we were wrong, promptly admitted it.

11. Sought through prayer and meditation to improve our

conscious contact with God as we understand Him, praying only for knowledge of His will for us and the power to carry that out.

12. Having had a spiritual awakening as a result of these steps, we tried to carry this message to alcoholics, and to practice these principles in all our affairs.

My personal thoughts, feelings, and experiences within Alcoholics Anonymous were suppressed on a number of occasions, and A.A. was not particularly fulfilling or supportive to me as an alcoholic free thinker. I had to "go it alone" for many years. But through it all, I kept my sobriety through prioritizing it on a day-to-day basis. There is no higher power keeping me sober. I make this choice and reacknowledge it daily. No one can do it for me.

Many nonreligious persons feel as I do. We are secularists and we choose life over an alcoholic existence that usually culminates in an alcohol-related death. We support each other while realizing that each of us is responsible for his or her own sobriety *no matter what*. Through having experienced years of full-blown alcoholism, our addiction potential is etched in our brains; active physiological addiction can remain arrested as long as we do not ingest mind-altering chemicals.

Grass-roots Secular Sobriety Groups offer an alternative or supplement to Alcoholics Anonymous, though both speak to this country's undisputed need for solutions to the lightning-speed growth of alcoholism and chemical dependency.

I had been sober almost nine years when I began to seriously consider the need for alternative secular groups that would utilize the sobriety priority rather than dependence upon a mystical higher power as the means to achieve and retain sobriety.

Free Inquiry magazine published an article in which I expressed my frustrations with A.A.'s religiosity and my belief that the needs of free thinkers are not being met there. My article received positive responses from alcoholic secularists across America. So I called my local parks-and-recreation department to inquire about the cost of renting a room one night a week.

Naturally, the person in charge asked why I wanted to rent the room. I said, "For the meetings of an alcoholism recovery support group." He pressed for the name of the group and, keeping my fingers crossed with the hope that he was not a strict religionist or a member of A.A., I said "We call ourselves the Secular Sobriety Group or S.S.G." Not knowing that I was at that time the only member of the group, he cordially answered, "That'll be fine. Have one of your people come on by and sign the forms for use of the room. I'll have to get approval, but that's just a formality. We have Monday nights free; how'll that be for you?" Since he'd ascertained that we were a small (ha!) grass-roots group, he arranged for the room to be ours on an ability-to-pay basis.

The first night I sat in the room alone. Since I don't believe in miracles, I did not really expect anyone to attend. True enough. A few days later I attended the most liberal A.A. meeting I could find, timidly passing around flyers afterward.

Two people attended the second S.S.G. meeting. One never returned. The other, an agnostic with a Jewish background, was quite fond of A.A. but felt that there was a genuine need for S.S.G.

For many weeks, despite attempts to spread the message with flyers and by word-of-mouth, that dear lady and I held most of the meetings for each other only. Once in a while a daring "heretic" would attend, eyes widening when he found no Higher Power or twelve steps to greet him. Human beings are by nature reluctant to leave something that works for them, even though it may contain elements that are repugnant to them or require the stifling of their better judgment. Alcoholics are especially afraid to try new approaches to sobriety, even if the approach they now use is tearing them apart. Who can blame them? I celebrate everyone's sobriety. I've been there. I've experienced the horrors of active alcoholism. I've gritted my teeth and said the Lord's prayer; after all, these A.A. people were *sober*. At one time, I too associated sobriety exclusively with A.A.

Since we had no money for expensive advertising, I began

to submit press releases to local daily metropolitan newspapers, weekly suburban newspapers, and local radio stations. Like most folks, I had other obligations and commitments, and a limited budget for Xeroxing and mailing; therefore I submitted releases only once a month. See Appendix B for more on press releases.

More weeks passed. Calls started coming more frequently on my home answering machine, sometimes several calls a day. I logged each call and the date, explaining to each person who called that S.S.G. was not anti-A.A. and that some of our members attended A.A. meetings as well. I also explained that all alcoholics were welcome to attend these free meetings, no matter what their belief system might be. However, I did stress that these meetings were secular, not religious, and that the majority of people attending considered themselves to be secular humanists or agnostics.

Among the many calls, I only received two negative responses. One was from a woman who shouted in my ear that people might be misled to think that S.S.G. was a branch of A.A., and one was from a man who said we'd better get our act together because if we believed in the universe we also believed in God, whether we knew it or not. There was also a supportive but strange call from a man who said he was behind us one-hundred percent and would like to send me some literature. A few days later a mailing arrived that described how aliens from another galaxy had beamed Jesus to earth.

More people began to attend our meetings. More weeks passed. A local radio station did a telephone interview with me about Secular Sobriety Groups. A local newspaper sent a reporter to our meeting and he did a favorable story on our group as well.

Meanwhile, *Free Inquiry*, after receiving favorable responses from around the nation regarding my article, published a piece by Donald Simmermacher entitled "A Humanistic Alternative to Alcoholics Anonymous." Portions of his article follow:

"Sobriety Without Superstition" by James Christopher (FI, Summer 1985) was a refreshing disclosure. As a civilian social worker for the U.S. Air Force Substance Abuse Rehabilitation Program, I am frequently involved with clients who share this view.

Alcoholics Anonymous (A.A.) is religious in nature, and its emphasis on public confession, acts of contrition, and divine intervention is well documented. Most who espouse the A.A. philosophy openly thwart any efforts to introduce more humanistic or secular approaches to the substance-abuse field.

. . . One of my greatest concerns is that A.A., as a religious organization, is being imposed upon individuals as a condition of substance-abuse treatment and rehabilitation. Mandatory attendance at A.A. meetings has become a common practice in treatment programs across the country.

. . . I have witnessed numerous cases in which A.A. has been imposed as a mandatory condition of alcohol-abuse rehabilitation. In one case, an individual was considered to have failed his treatment because of his resistance to attending A.A. and was removed from the Air Force. His prognosis was considered unfavorable because, as stated in the medical summary, "he was unable to find his *Higher Power*" (emphasis mine).

These cases represent just the tip of the iceberg. There are thousands of people forced to attend A.A. even though they do not respond to the religious approach of this self-help group.

. . . The *American Heritage Dictionary* defines "religion" as follows: "The expression of man's belief in a reverence for a super-human *power* recognized as the creator and governor of the universe . . . the spiritual or emotional attitude of one who recognizes the existence of a superhuman *power* or *powers*" (emphasis mine).

The A.A. process is guided by twelve steps. Six of the twelve clearly refer to the surrender to, or the dependency on, an external higher power.

. . . Anyone who has ever attended A.A. meetings is aware of the "Serenity Prayer" that is said at the beginning of each meeting. The prayer begins with the word "God." Acknowledgement of the existence of God requires belief in a superhuman or supernatural power. The second word of the prayer is "grant," which implies the belief that this *higher power* is a supernatural being or power who can bestow or give to lesser beings.

The book *Alcoholics Anonymous,* or the so-called Big Book, makes frequent reference to the need to believe in God, or a higher power, as a condition of maintaining sobriety and alcohol-abuse recovery.

Many other examples could be given to show that A.A. is indeed religious in nature. Its literature refers to "God," "Him," and "Higher Power." To argue, therefore, that A.A. does not require religious convictions is ludicrous.

. . . A.A. membership is estimated to be somewhere between half a million and one million members. Since there are an estimated ten to twelve million alcoholics in the United States, of them, many may be in need of an alternative recovery program.

. . . A.A. participants are not encouraged to become self-supporting or self-reliant. Their social life is often limited to making friends only with other alcoholics. Some disagree with the concept that members can never move beyond the A.A. group. It can be viewed as the substitution of chemicals for another kind of dependency—the continual A.A. group meeting that becomes a way of life.

. . . Since not all alcoholics or other *drug-abusers may respond favorably to A.A., there is a need to develop secular support groups that can act as alternatives for those who may not be religious.* . . . [Emphasis added.]

I was soon asked to write a second article for *Free Inquiry,* describing the S.S.G. meetings as a secular alternative to A.A. I began to receive many phone calls and letters, all in support of S.S.G. What follows are quotes gleaned from those responses:

I'm an alcoholic. And I was downright joyful to read the article about the Secular Sobriety Groups in *Free Inquiry.* . . . My secular humanism is a commitment that is hardwon and a very serious part of my own belief system, and the "humanist" A.A. meetings were actually more upsetting to me than just to stay home and apply the valid points of the A.A. program to myself for sobriety . . . I don't want to sit and listen to some good-intentioned sober person tell me about how I should just use the A.A. group as a higher power. I'm not interested in any higher power!!! I'm only interested in staying sober as a humanist, *not* as a theist, and I find all the religiously oriented regimens of A.A. meetings very disturbing and counterproductive to my own program of sobriety. . . . Most mainstream A.A. members are convinced one cannot stay sober and enjoy life without being some variety of Christian or believer. The *Free Inquiry* article and news of S.S.G. gives me new hope.

I just read your article in *Free Inquiry* and I agree with you 100%. I've attended some meetings of O.A. (Overeaters Anonymous), which is based on A.A. and uses the Big Book and other literature of Alcoholics Anonymous, and I find the religious aspect to be more than I can take. . . . I mentioned your group (S.S.G.) at one of our meetings. This group is O.A./A.A. and [is for] cross-addicted persons. I expressed my problem with the higher power stuff and several others in the group shared the same feelings. Some said they'd be interested in forming a local Secular Sobriety Group.

I am an "active" alcoholic who has been half-heartedly seeking sobriety through A.A. drug treatment centers (with mandatory A.A. attendance). . . . I don't know what I am . . . except a drunk who wishes he were sober. A.A. acquaintances assure me that it's simply a question of my not having hit whatever my "bottom" is to be and that when, inevitably, I do, adherence to the precepts of A.A. will come easily and naturally. Perhaps they are right, but it terrifies me to contemplate how much further down I will have to sink before this occurs . . . and that my "bottom" might be death or irrevocable insanity.

I am a twenty-four-year-old, recently recovering alcoholic. I've always considered myself . . . a secular humanist. I've been seeking support from a local hospital and A.A.—both of which insist upon using God to solve one's alcoholism and every other personal imperfection—as you have already discovered. Needless to say, I've found this form of counseling relatively useless. I was delighted to learn of your group through *Free Inquiry*.

I currently attend A.A. meetings and even though I have managed not to drink in 30 months, there are certain aspects of [A.A.'s] teachings that I cannot accept. There is one meeting that specifically caters to agnostics but that doesn't seem to fit the bill because, as you probably know, A.A. feels that the agnostic will eventually "come to believe."

. . . I am not a believer in God or any other higher power in the A.A. sense, and that fact has caused me a *lot* of trouble in A.A., so much so [that] at times the difficulty and the feeling that "I don't fit" in A.A. have jeopardized the little sobriety I have. Despite the A.A. disclaimers, it seems to me that those (such as myself) who do not believe in a higher power as a necessity for sobriety do not fit well in Alcoholics Anonymous. Nevertheless, it almost seems as if A.A. is "the only game in town" for those of us who perceive the [need] for a recovery support group.

. . . I am a secular humanist and I am also an alcoholic. I have nine years of sobriety. But it has been a hard go. I tried A.A. off and on for years and years. But I was very frustrated with all of their higher-power philosophy. I would stay sober for long periods of time, then I would go to an A.A. meeting, and right after these meetings I would go out and get drunk. So A.A. was really worse for me than nothing at all.

I have been concerned about a family member's drinking for some time, but have never before found any support group or treatment center I could even suggest. This person feels very strongly about the mysticism associated with any religon, and I know this person would not have anything to do with A.A.

I am very impressed with the rational intelligence and ethical sensitivity of S.S.G.'s approach. "Ahh, at last, minds I could communicate with, people whose judgment I could respect." Since repudiating Christian religiosity was a primary act of self-liberation and ethical choice in adolescence, I found A.A. so offensive as to be unusable— not even a port in a storm. I've never felt more alienated in my life than at their meetings or when trying to communicate my objections to the twelve-step program to a counselor trained to work hand-in-glove with A.A.

As a humanist I strongly believe in the strengths of the individual. I firmly believe in the resources of the *informed* person against addiction. I certainly understand that the condition (and it is a disease process, *not* an outcome of failures of moral development) *can* reach the point where people need outside help even to realize what has been happening to them and break the cycle. However, once people get help, recognize the illness, I believe that reason, persistence—all the tools of the mind—used to actively search out and find whatever helps the individual—not blindly following someone else's X-step program—will work. In any case it's been working for me this last year and a half.

In one of your articles you mentioned the difficulty of breaking away from A.A. (the grateful syndrome), or questioning, dissenting within A.A. It's not surprising that that's hard to do. The program *teaches* learned helplessness, dependency, a non-questioning (humble) cast of mind.

What I would tell people is "Yes, you have developed this illness. This addictive condition will always be a potential risk for you. Your body needs treatment and support. Your life may have to be put back in order, but there are people who will support you, and many, many things you can do to help yourself. *You* have resources. You're *not* helpless and you're *not* guilty."

Our Secular Sobriety Group meeting is an hour and a half long. Socializing, snacking, and exchanging viewpoints and phone numbers before and after the meeting are enhanced by soft classical music from a portable cassette player. The meeting is informal and each week a different person is asked to act as moderator. He or she sets the tone for the meeting by reading aloud a short selection of his or her choice from secular literature related to alcoholism. Humanistic inspirational selections, taken from the works of free thinkers, are read on occasion as well.

Our S.S.G. literature table displays not only articles and books related to alcoholism, but also various free-thought publications to help strengthen the alcoholic's thinking abilities in sobriety. (See Appendix C for a list of reference sources for materials pertaining to alcoholism and recovery and also of secular-humanist organizations and publications that promote skeptical thinking and provide sources for networking with persons of like mind.) The rational mind, the sober, undrugged brain is an alcoholic's best tool for making clear choices and keeping one's life priorities straight, not muddled by drugs or religion.

The moderator either picks a topic or opens the meeting to general discussion. Feelings, thoughts, family problems, etc., are kept in confidence. At the end of the meeting, someone usually closes with a short humanistic reading.

A suggested opening for a Secular Sobriety Group meeting goes something like this:

Facilitator: "Hello everyone, and welcome to the Monday night meeting of the Secular Sobriety Group. We are an autonomous grass-roots gathering of sober alcoholics and friends and families of alcoholics. The primary purpose of our group is to support individuals who wish to achieve and maintain sobriety. We define sobriety as abstinence from alcohol and drugs. We also strive to grow as persons, to experience life on a high, human level, free from mind-altering chemicals. As secularists we do not base our sobriety upon the intervention of a mystical or supernatural higher power. As humanists, we reach out to one another in human love, dealing directly with our human problems.

"We are not anti-A.A.; some of our members attend A.A. meetings, some do not. We celebrate every alcoholic's sobriety."

The facilitator may choose to read a brief selection from secular inspirational literature, and then continue:

"Everything we share here tonight is to be kept in confidence. Please respect the needs of those who wish to speak by limiting your sharing-time. Let's go 'round the table and introduce ourselves. I'm Vera, your facilitator for tonight's meeting, and I'm a sober alcoholic."

Members usually acknowledge by responding with "Hi, Vera." Introductions are made and the discussion begins. Those who do not wish to speak can simply pass. There may be a coffee break. At the end of the meeting, the facilitator closes with another secular reading and then says:

"Thank you all for being a part of our meeting tonight. There are refreshments—coffee, tea, and snacks—in the kitchen. Feel free to indulge. S.S.G. has neither dues nor fees. We are self-supporting through our own contributions. There is a basket on the table for this purpose. I encourage you to exchange phone numbers, especially if you are newly sober. Pick up the phone instead of a drink. Thank you again and we'll see you next week."

This meeting structure is only a suggestion; secular gatherings, brimming with free thinkers, take on their own tone. And we've found that simply being in the company of other nontheist alcoholics and the absence of religiosity are liberating and help to build and maintain recovery from alcoholism.

As our grass-roots group grew, we received calls and letters not only from alcoholics but also from concerned nonalcoholic family members, lovers, friends, employers, therapists, etc. One of our nonalcoholic members occasionally holds meetings for families and friends of alcoholics in an adjacent room in our facility on the same evening. On other evenings he and other nonalcoholics share our common problem during our regular meetings. This has proven supportive for all of us. We grow as persons, expressing our love and care as well as our angers and frustrations; therefore, nonalcoholic support groups have evolved, offering an alternative/supplement to Al-Anon meetings (the nonalcoholics' version of A.A.). In traditional Al-Anon meetings, A.A.'s twelve steps are used.

In our meetings for nonalcoholics, some find a secularized version of the twelve steps useful; others do not. In the Secular Sobriety Group meetings, some of our members find secularized versions of these steps useful, as a framework for living; others have, instead, created their own programs, abandoning the steps altogether; still others utilize a blend, taking the best from a variety of sources.

For example, at least one group uses these six suggested guidelines:

1. To break the cycle of denial and achieve sobriety, we first acknowledge that *we are alcoholics.*
2. We *reaffirm* this truth daily and accept without reservation—one day at a time—the fact that, as sober alcoholics, we cannot and do not drink, *no matter what.*
3. Since drinking is not an option for us, we take whatever steps are necessary to continue our sobriety priority lifelong.
4. A high quality of life—the good life—can be achieved. However, life is also filled with uncertainties; therefore, we do not drink regardless of feelings, circumstances, or conflicts.
5. We share in confidence with each other our thoughts and feelings as sober alcoholics.
6. Sobriety is our priority and we are each individually responsible for our lives and our sobriety.

The bottom line for alcoholics is staying sober. Growth is important too, however; alcoholics and nonalcoholics alike must strive to become better, happier persons, lead more fruitful lives, choose more fulfilling (and less destructive) behaviors, and deal with emotions without superstition, emerging from the existentialist void with our reasoning muscles flexed and our intimacy bondings balanced. All this makes for clearer perspectives toward the realities of living.

To illustrate what a Secular Sobriety Group meeting is like, in contrast to the more traditional A.A. meeting, I offer two hypothetical scenarios:

Believer's Version, Including Higher Power

"Hi, I'm Sally and I'm an alcoholic."

Group responds: "Hi, Sally!"

Sally continues: "I really didn't want to come here tonight, but I guess my Higher Power felt I needed a meeting, so here

I am. I had a really big fight with my boss today. I feel bad about it but I guess I've got to turn it over to my Higher Power. I've been sober for a little over six months now."

The group applauds and encourages her to continue with "Atta girl, Sally," "Ha! That's it Sally!" etc.

Sally goes on: "You people have really made me realize what love and caring can be. I've been trying to work the steps and haven't got very far yet, but I keep trying. If it weren't for you people and my Higher Power, I know I'd be right back out there again on my face in some bar. I don't have the strength to do it on my own. My Higher Power must be taking care of me, holding me close. Sometimes when I'm alone at night my Higher Power calms me down. It works. These steps and these principles work. I told my A.A. sponsor yesterday that sometimes I doubt— maybe that's not the right word—sometimes I want things too fast, things that my Higher Power feels are not for my own good. I listen to my sponsor, most times. Sometimes I think she's full of it and I want to rebel, go my own way, but I know I need this. I need her help. She's been sober for a long time and I know she knows what she's talking about. I've started going back to my old church. When I was drinking I used to curse God. Now I'm willing to surrender.

"My best thinking got me here. I try not to let my crazy head tell me what to do. I just put one foot in front of the other and take one step at a time, one day at a time. My boyfriend is getting along better now with my little girl. God is disclosing more and more to me each day. It's a relief to just 'let go and let God.' I called my mom two days ago. We cried. She's so pleased that I'm going to church again and that I'm sober now. I wasn't going to share this tonight, but Paul (my boyfriend) keeps insisting that I pack up and move in with him. I don't feel ready for that just yet. I need more time in sobriety. Paul's a nonalcholic. He says he loves me but when we talk I get confused. He screws around with my thinking. He respects my A.A. program and all, but he's not a believer. My sponsor said I should picture God as I understand him, not punishing and harsh, like I was taught, but caring and loving and powerful. Somehow Paul may come to believe.

I know I can't change him, but I think I really love him. Anyway, thank you all for being here and 'keep coming back.'"

The group responds with applause and cheerful hoots.

Heretical Version, Free from Higher Power

"Hi, I'm Sally and I'm an alcoholic."

Group responds: "Hi, Sally!"

Sally continues: "I really didn't want to come here tonight, but I felt I needed a meeting, so here I am. I had a really big fight with my boss today. I feel bad about it. I guess I've got a right to my feelings, but I don't have to dwell on them.

"I've been sober for a little over six months now."

The group applauds and encourges her to continue with "Atta girl, Sally," "Ha! That's it Sally!" etc.

Sally goes on: "You people have really made me realize what love and caring can be. If it weren't for my choosing each day to prioritize my sobriety *no matter what* and the encouragement of you people I know I'd be right back out there again on my face in some bar. Now I'm willing to surrender to the fact that I am an alcoholic and each day I feel a little bit better, and a little bit stronger.

"My boyfriend is getting along better now with my little girl. I called my mom two days ago. We cried. She's proud of me. I feel better about myself, too. I wasn't going to share this tonight, but Paul (my boyfriend) keeps insisting that I pack up and move in with him. I don't feel ready for that just yet. I need more time in sobriety.

"Paul's a nonalcholic. He says he loves me but I want to be really sure of my feelings and more secure in myself before making a commitment. I think I really love him. Anyway, thanks for listening."

The group responds with applause and cheerful hoots.

Please note that the second version gets to the heart of the matter without being couched in religious rhetoric. Heretical Sally has problems in living, newly sober, as does Believer Sally; but if something unusually stress-producing is introduced into the lives of both Sallys, Believer Sally may call her A.A. sponsor—and may well find her drunk or out of town. Believer Sally will pray to God and, for whatever reasons, may not feel God respond. She is in the muddled mental territory of religion plus trauma minus rationality. Believer Sally, who never stated her priority of sobriety *no matter what*, might be more likely to revert back to drinking than Heretical Sally, who, at the very least, tends to have some perspective on real life without gods and goblins. Heretical Sally, newly sober, is as subject to overreacting to stress as is Believer Sally, but is clear on the fact that when all else goes bananas she still has her sobriety priority, one day at a time. Religion does not get in the way or cloud the issue of her priority. Her Secular Sobriety Group may individually or collectively disappoint her—they might even for some strange reason board a bus for Toledo, leaving no forwarding address. A hurricane may destroy her home, her mother may suddenly go insane, her boyfriend might introduce her to his new boyfriend, but she still has her sobriety, *if* she continues to prioritize it daily. And as time passes, with reasonable effort, she'll develop new coping skills in living sober, unhampered by religious dogma. Believer Sally could come out of the aforementioned events sober also if, in that crisis moment, she puts her sobriety before the whims of her God.

Which Sally would you lay odds on?

Okay, my argument could be construed as being somewhat slanted. But time and again I have seen free thinkers give in, by their own admission, to bad feelings experienced early on, rather than hanging in there by prioritizing sobriety. After years of being told over and over by A.A. religionists that they must find a higher power to stay sober, many succumb to peer pressure.

Again, A.A. helps multitudes of alcoholics. Secular alternative groups can help nonreligious alcoholics. Human life is at stake here; A.A. speaks its mind, in print and in practice. Free thinkers have the same right.

S.S.G. members get to the heart of the matter in our meetings. Religion and higher powers don't get in the way of our recovery and we are not dependent upon these will-o'-the-wisps for our sobriety.

We hope also to grow as persons in these dogma-free meetings, learning from the experiences of other sober alcoholics. As you might imagine, there's very little preaching; freethinkers generally don't tolerate that sort of approach for too long.

Grass-roots Secular Sobriety Groups are forming across the nation, providing a needed alternative for nonreligious persons. If there's no such group in your area and you cannot start one, use the suggestions in this book to help you survive with your identity intact within the fellowship of Alcoholics Anonymous. Or perhaps you simply cannot tolerate the A.A. approach. That's okay. You've got plenty of company. *Just don't drink.* You now have the opportunity to choose to stay sober each day, one day at at time, lifelong. It is not a matter of willpower. Honestly setting your priorities is your key to the sober life.

22 Maintaining Sobriety

Sobriety is achieved by the individual alcoholic, sometimes alone, but most typically with the initial intervention and support of family, friends, and/or alcoholism professionals; the initial detoxification period, which usually lasts a few days, is best spent within the confines of a protective environment such as a hospital clinic, and may be aided by the controlled use of tranquilizers.

After this initial withdrawal period, the alcoholic faces (1) staying sober or (2) an eventual alcohol-related death. Maintaining abstinence from alcohol and other mind-altering drugs is best achieved through the daily sobriety priority. The sobriety priority is a separate issue and must remain intact lifelong on a daily basis *as a separate issue*. The sobriety priority is just that: the priority; it need not be an obsession.

The ability to *choose* can be restored only in sobriety. Non-alcoholics do not choose to control their drinking. Their drinking physiology is, for the most part, on automatic pilot. For the alcoholic, drinking takes on a life of its own.

For alcoholics, however, sobriety never goes on automatic pilot and never takes on a life of its own, and to think so is a tragic illusion.

Once sober, it is the individual alcoholic's responsiblity to maintain sobriety. This is accomplished by acknowledging daily the life-and-death necessity of staying sober. The sobriety priority is a separate issue, not based on any other issue or on how one may feel about oneself, one's circumstances, or one's significant others at any given time. As long as the sober alcoholic lets nothing get in the way of sobriety, be it a belief, conflict, event, feeling, or thought, and as long as one retains the sobriety priority, reaffirmed daily as the core issue of his or her very being, sobriety can be maintained lifelong. One cannot relive the past or reverse one's physiology, magically switching from an alcoholic body to a non-alcoholic body. Longtime, lifetime sobriety for alcoholics is achieved and re-achieved each day after the initial experience of sobriety.

The alcoholism experience cannot be known by nonalcoholics. They cannot truly feel it or empathize with it. The alcoholism experience is stored permanently in the cerebral cortexes of alcoholics through behaviors repeated over and over again during many waking hours. It cannot be unexperienced.

Chronic experiences leave their mark, literally. Clinical studies done in the 1950s by Wilder Penfield, a Canadian neurosurgeon, demonstrated this vividly; Penfield electrically stimulated selected spots of the cerebral cortexes of his patients, evoking a variety of memory responses when he did so. There is no surgical eraser or correction fluid to blot out our experiences, save death; therefore we remember.

At certain times in life, nothing seems to be going right. But even when the sober alcoholic's career, love life, or cherished goals are at times unsatisfactory, there is still sobriety to count as the most single positive aspect of his life. It can and must be maintained through whatever circumstances, feelings, and conflicts he may encounter.

On this simple construct one can light and rekindle daily the flame for a lifetime of continuous sobriety. Denial in other areas of one's life may remain intact indefinitely. One may sometimes dislike oneself or one's circumstances. One may choose to sit on the bleachers of life and simply observe. One may be more intro-verted than most, more depressed than most, receive more of life's notoriously unfair blows than most, and yet remain sober through it all, if one acknowledges daily that, above all else, in spite of everything, he or she is an alcoholic who does not drink *no matter what.*

This daily vigilance of one's sobriety priority will link day to day and year to year with the passage of time; however, the accumulation of sober time achieved will not insure against a future relapse as, again, there is no automatic pilot here.

For this simple construct to work—and it does, without belief in a higher power—one's sobriety must be viewed as a continuing, separate issue, every day, lifelong.

In sobriety, the alcoholism experience, the physiological addiction, is a "sleeping giant." Go beyond this experience and let the sleeping giant lie, one day at a time.

23 Across-the-Board Sobriety

Members of S.S.G. in the Los Angeles area and across the country have been very supportive; their valuable insights and necessary input have resulted in the growth of a secular alternative, not only for alcoholics, but also for the families and friends of alcoholics and other chemically dependant persons who are seeking sobriety. Groups have been formed to help those addicted to cocaine, heroin, speed (amphetamines), marijuana, and other drugs, as well as cigarette smokers and persons with eating disorders, sexual problems, compulsive gamblers, etc. These Secular Support Groups are addressing people's needs with a secular approach free from religious dogma.

One S.S.G. member who had been off cocaine for almost three years with the help of Alcoholics Anonymous and Cocaine Anonymous shared with us that he not only found it hard to relate to religious persons and their "God admonitions" but also had trouble relating to alcoholics, since he had been addicted exclusively to cocaine, not alcohol. He had always been a moderate drinker. Alcohol had posed no problems or threats to his rather successful lifestyle. When cocaine entered the picture, however, he eventually lost everything: his booming business, his home, his relationship, his money. He pointed out that, although he could not relate to alcoholics as an alcoholic, he *could* relate to sobriety and his need to prioritize sobriety in his life. Once free from active addiction to cocaine, he also chose not to drink for a very logical reason: though he was not an alcoholic, he realised that he was vulnerable while under the influence of alcohol, and his drinking could leave him open to his cocaine addiction. So even though he has no history of alcoholism, he steers clear of alcohol and all other mind-altering drugs as well, to avoid the possibility of an eventual relapse into cocaine addiction. He does not identify himself as an alcoholic yet he chooses not to drink. Variations on this and other related themes abound as S.S.G. members choose sobriety *no matter what*.

When life is at stake, one with a history of addiction to any mind-altering chemical does well to steer clear of other mind-altering chemicals as well. Choosing across-the-board sobriety may be the better path, even if one is not necessarily susceptible to the phenomenon of cross-addiction and has a history of harmless moderate use of one or more of these chemicals. Forging a new history in sobriety protects addicts. If some see this as overkill, let them cast the first shot glass or syringe.

24 Alcoholics Helping Alcoholics

> Don't walk in front of me
> I may not follow
> Don't walk behind me
> I may not lead
> Walk beside me
> And just be my friend
> —Albert Camus

That's how A.A. began, really; two alcoholics supporting each other by staying sober day to day.

Some old timers recalled the early days of Alcoholics Anonymous for me. They said that back in those days alcoholics made "twelfth-step calls" (based on A.A.'s twelfth step of carrying the message to other suffering alcoholics) even before A.A. had written the twelve steps. Sober alcoholics would seek out other alcoholics in hospital settings or by word of mouth. The sober alcoholics would visit the ones they felt had hit bottom, those who were "sick and tired of being sick and tired." They would relay the message of A.A. whenever and wherever they found an opportunity to do so. They would help to "detox" alcoholics and nurse them through withdrawal and D.T.s (delirium tremens or "the horrors," hallucinations and uncontrollable shakes suffered during acute withdrawal from alcohol).

One of these old timers said that Bill Wilson, A.A.'s co-founder, would carry a Bible with him and tell a prospective newcomer to get down on his knees and pray with him.

Today's communities are overcrowded, and there is less human contact. Also, since most communities now have chemical dependency wards staffed with alcoholism professionals to administer to the needs of alcoholics in the initial stage of detox, A.A. is not in the detox business today and that's probably just as well. However, A.A. is still in the religion business and in the people business. A.A. sponsorship is still practiced, that is, one person with a longer time in sobriety sponsors or guides a newer person. The implications are obvious. Some sponsors are heavy-handed gurus; others use a lighter, friendship approach.

I recall a couple of sponsors I had when I was newly sober and attending A.A. meetings. My first sponsor took my fifth step with me; together we "admitted to God, to ourselves, and to another human being, the exact nature of our wrongs." After I had confessed, pouring my heart out to him, he told me that "it takes a long time for all of us (alcoholics) to grow up."

My second sponsor informed me that "we probably became alcoholics due to something we did in our past lives" (referring to reincarnation).

In sobriety I think we'd do well to avoid sponsorship, approaching each other as equals, walking side by side.

Alcoholics helping alcoholics on an equal basis can be a rewarding experience. We needn't sponsor each other. We can share our feelings and thoughts with each other and just be there when an alcoholic is feeling low and needs a sober alcoholic to talk with.

Personally I find it pointless to talk with another alcoholic when he is under the influence. I always tell a drinking alcoholic this and invite him to call me back in the morning when he is sober. I have a right to my own life and my own time. I am not a rescuer. I am not a savior, nor am I an evangelist.

In early sobriety it is especially helpful to keep busy, to get out of oneself, so to speak. Helping other alcoholics is one way to accomplish this, to build sober time for oneself. Compassion is a powerful motivator but it is wise to strike a balance as well. It is not always easy to do so, however.

Several years ago I heard a very frightened, suffering, newly sober alcoholic express a literal cry for help at a traditional A.A. meeting.

He had had twenty-four hours of sobriety. He begged someone—anyone—to help him through the night until he could sign himself into a halfway house on the other side of town.

Having been ejected from his mother's apartment, he'd been sleeping secretly in the boiler room below. Not being a regular at this particular meeting, I waited around and listened. After the meeting ended, a few members gave him the party line, smiled reassuringly, winked, and left. I chose to intervene.

After checking him into a nearby hotel room and giving him my phone number, I took him to a midnight meeting. The following morning I returned and drove him to the halfway house, since he had no car. Later I heard that he'd opted for staying sober in his own neighborhood and that he had been reunited with his family. During that first evening I had told him "You are precious. You have one life to live. The choice is yours, the rest is bullshit." Years later I ran into him at a local laundromat. He was still sober and seemed fine.

I believe that he had grasped the truth of his preciousness, his right to live. Did he thank me for my help that night? Nope. Did my intervention, my giving a damn, pay off? I'll never really know. The scenario could have been different. In reality *he* took the steps and is apparently still taking the steps, maintaining his sober condition. I was not his savior, but it made me feel good to see one more life escape needless suffering.

A few nights ago I was awakened by my answering machine. Stumbling to the phone, I picked up the receiver. A lady's voice on the other end said she was sorry if she woke me but she wanted to know about Secular Sobriety Groups. I told her that if she'd call back on the following day I'd be happy to give her information about the meetings.

I glanced at the clock on my way back to bed. It was 3:30 A.M. Perhaps this person had called me in an alcoholic blackout, perhaps not. She chose not to call me back the following day.

Helping other alcoholics is a personal choice, not a prerequisite for sobriety. Many times I'm involved with projects that have nothing whatsoever to do with alcoholism, and I have a right to my own interests.

As a sober alcoholic, I have received personal fulfillment and emotional enrichment from being a friend (within reason) to other alcoholics. Unlike A.A., however, I see no cosmic carrots on mystical sticks.

25 Sobriety Comes Out of the Closet

I've had the privilege to speak with hundreds of other sober alcoholics across the nation, nontheists all. These nonreligious people are staying sober *without* belief in a higher power, mystical or secularized, and many without the utilization of A.A.'s twelve steps. Those with long-term sobriety all have something in common: *the sobriety priority*.

I've questioned and researched for a number of years now why some alcoholics maintain their sobriety and others do not. I have reached a conclusion that I feel is quite sound and reasonable but by no means original: Alcoholics who practice daily and adhere to their individual sobriety priority *no matter what* stay sober for the long term; the others simply do not, whether or not they believe in God.

This was summed up nicely for me in a recent phone conversation with a sober alcoholic inquiring about Secular Sobriety Groups. She related to me that both she and her husband had had several years of sobriety. Her husband had pushed his alcoholism into the closet, kept it to himself, even halfway denied it on occasion, whereas she prioritized her sobriety daily, maintaining her awareness daily to herself, sharing this openly with other people whenever possible. She is still sober; he, unfortunately, is not. They are both nontheists.

This emphasis on one's sobriety priority cuts across barriers of belief or nonbelief, age, personality, length of sobriety, etc. Even religious long-time sober alcoholics put their individual sobriety priority before their God when the chips are down, in their heart of hearts, in flash moments of clarity demanding hard choices. Most religionists would not easily admit this but some have shared it with me. Only a small numer of believers have revealed it straight out—most have coupled the revelation with mental gymnastics to quell the guilt of having momentarily side-stepped their God in order to stay sober. After all, many religionists believe that their God might feel it best, for reasons beyond our human understanding, that believers experience alcoholism to experience growth as persons. Hence, it's really refreshing when a religious alcoholic shares that the sobriety priority comes first in his or her daily life.

Sometimes this is accomplished by crediting the deity with giving Mr. or Ms. Believer the strength and insight to prioritize sobriety above all else (including the deity). Admittedly, it gets a bit confusing. As a nontheist, the muddy waters of religion long ago parted for me. I can see reality with a good deal more clarity and it offers me safer ground on which to stand in life.

Standing one's ground isn't all sobriety is about, though. Experiencing life on its own terms, sober, is the only way I can survive and have a life, any life—hopefully the good life. As long as my addiction to the chemical in question is not reignited by my failing, for even just one day, to prioritize my sobriety above all else, the good life is within reach. This priority allows alcoholics to live and is obviously the way of life necessary to avoid "required drinking" or physiological addiction, which triggers learned behavior patterns and emotional responses related to drinking.

The sobriety priority is the safest, sanest approach to life for a sober addict. One's life may be very productive or not so productive. That is entirely up to one's limitations, efforts and circumstances.

As I stated earlier, for an alcoholic to accumulate a string of consecutive sober days, weeks, months, years—a lifetime of sobriety—is in and of itself the ultimate goal. It is an achievement that not only benefits the sober alcoholic and allows him to participate in life to whatever degree he is willing and capable, but obviously benefits society as well.

When human beings look back upon their lives, they always find that some things were left undone, loves unrequited, goals unachieved; but, if we alcoholics have maintained our sobriety by keeping it prioritized, is that not a grand accomplishment? We have left our previous sub-human state behind and lived our lives one day at a time, with our physiological addiction dormant.

Being open about one's alcoholism, referring to oneself as a sober alcoholic, and sharing one's sobriety date, are healthy, up-front awareness-builders that may help and encourage others but, most important, help keep us conscious of our individual sobriety priority.

I have rarely encountered resistance or shock from the alcoholics or nonalcholics with whom I've shared my situation. Almost everyone I've met in my sober years has told me of a relative, spouse or close friend who is an alcoholic. Alcoholism is rampant in our culture. Remember, approximately ten percent of our population is alcoholic—via physiological addiction, not character defects. We are who we are and our *no-matter-what* sobriety is nothing to be ashamed of. Corpses, on the other hand, are also never ashamed. Active alcoholism imprisons us, yet, through sobriety prioritized, we are set free to truly live our lives.

26 Conclusion

Recently I helped a nonalcoholic psychologist friend bring one of his colleagues home from a local hospital. She had voluntarily hospitalized herself for suicidal depression. Only a few evenings earlier, a sober alcoholic had shared at a Secular Sobriety Group meeting that, in the five years he'd been sober, he'd never experienced despair in any real way.

Sure, he'd experienced hard times, he said, and had felt low on occasion, but, thanks to his commitment to his sobriety priority and the self-esteem resulting from his living sober, he had never experienced suicidal hopelessness and helplessness.

I can relate to that. Probably all human beings have felt, as did Jean-Paul Sartre, anguish from "the human condition." I know I have. Perhaps, as some biographers have noted, at least part of Sartre's anguish was drug-induced. I know at least part of mine was.

The onslaught of acute psychic pain and suffering is sometimes why alcoholics and nonalcoholics alike reach for alcohol or other drugs. They believe it will relieve their anguish and they will experience better living through chemistry. Alcoholics, however, can't let go of the bottle because of their physiological addiction. Thus begins the vicious cycle of their anguish and despair.

Glancing back at my earlier drinking days (as it's not polite to stare), I recall my own suicide attempt in the early 1970s. Addictive drinking had become a way of life for me by then.

Swept along by my full-blown alcoholism, I attended a gathering where imbibing was a matter of course, our reason for being. At this party full of liberated souls, I saw my life as one long unending soap opera. Peering dreamily at a fellow approaching me in a white caftan, I took some of the valium that was being passed around like candy and washed it down with natural wine.

Operating within this colorful milieu, I decided to make my previously idle threats of suicide a reality.

When I left the party it all seemed clear to me: Life had not gone my way, a recent love affair had ended, and now I had the "courage" to end it all. I drove to a local drug store and purchased a six pack of soda pop and two hundred nonprescription sleeping pills.

I sat in the passenger side of my car and proudly managed to systematically swallow all the pills. Then I locked my car and walked to a nearby pay phone to say goodbye to (and get sympathy from) a friend who was in one of my psychotherapy groups.

When my friend heard my barely audible, pre-death speech, he began to sob openly. Something registered in my fading consciousness.

"I want to live," I said. Dropping the pay-phone receiver, I staggered toward a surreal area of light. Still standing, I spotted a slowly moving police car. "I've . . . taken . . . ovah . . . overdose. Help. Please help me." An officer in the car replied, "There's a hospital near here, just keep walking." Then he sped away.

Somehow I managed to blink away blurring vision and walk approximately a block, cement-like step after step, to what appeared to be a hospital entrance.

With all the will to survive I could muster, I made it into the corridor to tell someone, anyone, what had now become apparent. I was dying.

A doctor emerged, put his hand on my shoulder, and walked me toward an emergency room. As we walked he asked me what I'd ingested. What happened next is rather vague in my memory.

I do remember a lot of things being done to me, lifesaving

measures during which I was beyond feeling physical pain. Medical personnel took turns gently slapping my face and asking my name and address over and over again. Even under the circumstances, I could tell it was touch and go. I kept repeating, "I want to live. Will I live?"

Finally I got an answer from a kindly black woman, shortly before I was allowed to pass out. She looked me in the eye with a love I'll never forget and said, "Honey, yes, you'll live, and don't you ever put that shit in your body again. Don't you do that to yourself ever again."

So I take this opportunity to say to you, if you are having serious problems with alcohol or other drugs, if your life has become unmanageable, if you're thinking of checking out, and if these thoughts and feelings are becoming deeper by the day: "Honey, you can choose to live, one day at a time. You can choose sobriety." Although I made no more attempts at suicide, I continued to drink for a few more years after that incident. *You* don't have to.

And, if you've already been sober a few days or a few years, think of the useless, drug-induced misery you are avoiding as you leave the depths of despair behind, having chosen sobriety.

As you experience feelings and behaviors sober, you'll only have to occasionally contend with a fading Pavlovian pull. As long as you acknowledge your alcoholism and/or drug addiction *daily* and prioritzie your sobriety *daily,* you *will not* have to contend with "chemically required" drinking or drug-use, simply by not taking that first drink, smoking that first joint, snorting that first line of coke, or popping that first pill.

And, as a free thinker, you can choose not to credit your self-esteem to a mythical higher power. In crediting yourself for your ongoing achievement of sobriety, you can build a positive cycle of being, by not giving your self-esteem away to something or someone else.

Appendix A
Weekly Journal

The weekly journal on pages 131-183 will allow you to jot down the thoughts and feelings you experience in your first year of sobriety. Whether or not you choose to continue your journal after the first year, it remains crucial that you continue to acknowledge daily your arrested addiction and reaffirm your sobriety priority.

WEEK 1: __/__/__ to __/__/__

It hurts, but it will get better. I trust in time's healing process. I will not drink today!

Sunday. My name is _____ and I am a _____.
I do not _____ *no matter what.* I prioritize my _____ above all else.

_____

_____

Monday. My name is _____ and I am a _____.
I do not _____ *no matter what.* I prioritize my _____ above all else.

_____

_____

Tuesday. My name is _____ and I am a _____.
I do not _____ *no matter what.* I prioritize my _____ above all else.

_____

_____

Wednesday. My name is _____ and I am a _____.
I do not _____ *no matter what.* I prioritize my _____ above all else.

_____

_____

Thursday. My name is _____ and I am a _____.
I do not _____ *no matter what.* I prioritize my _____ above all else.

_____

_____

Friday. My name is _____ and I am a _____.
I do not _____ *no matter what.* I prioritize my _____ above all else.

_____

_____

Saturday. My name is _____ and I am a _____.
I do not _____ *no matter what.* I prioritize my _____ above all else.

_____

_____

Congratulations! You have achieved your first week of sobriety!

WEEK 2: __/__/__ to __/__/__

Today is all we have. I won't drink it away.

Sunday. My name is _____ and I am a _____.
I do not _____ *no matter what.* I prioritize my _____ above all else.
_____

_____

Monday. My name is _____ and I am a _____.
I do not _____ *no matter what.* I prioritize my _____ above all else.
_____

_____

Tuesday. My name is _____ and I am a _____.
I do not _____ *no matter what.* I prioritize my _____ above all else.
_____

_____

Wednesday. My name is _____ and I am a _____.
I do not _____ *no matter what.* I prioritize my _____ above all else.
_____

_____

Thursday. My name is _____ and I am a _____.
I do not _____ *no matter what.* I prioritize my _____ above all else.
_____

_____

Friday. My name is _____ and I am a _____.
I do not _____ *no matter what.* I prioritize my _____ above all else.
_____

_____

Saturday. My name is _____ and I am a _____.
I do not _____ *no matter what.* I prioritize my _____ above all else.
_____

_____

Congratulations! You have achieved your second week of sobriety!

WEEK 3: __/__/__ to __/__/__

In sobriety I have the power of choice. I won't drink today.

Sunday. My name is _____ and I am a _____.
I do not _____ *no matter what.* I prioritize my _____ above all else.

_____

_____

Monday. My name is _____ and I am a _____.
I do not _____ *no matter what.* I prioritize my _____ above all else.

_____

_____

Tuesday. My name is _____ and I am a _____.
I do not _____ *no matter what.* I prioritize my _____ above all else.

_____

_____

Wednesday. My name is _____ and I am a _____.
I do not _____ *no matter what.* I prioritize my _____ above all else.

_____

_____

Thursday. My name is _____ and I am a _____.
I do not _____ *no matter what.* I prioritize my _____ above all else.

_____

_____

Friday. My name is _____ and I am a _____.
I do not _____ *no matter what.* I prioritize my _____ above all else.

_____

_____

Saturday. My name is _____ and I am a _____.
I do not _____ *no matter what.* I prioritize my _____ above all else.

_____

_____

Congratulations! You have achieved your third week of sobriety!

WEEK 4: __/__/__ to __/__/__

Today I breathe the fresh air of my sobriety.

Sunday. My name is _____ and I am a _____.
I do not _____ *no matter what.* I prioritize my _____ above all else.

_____

_____

Monday. My name is _____ and I am a _____.
I do not _____ *no matter what.* I prioritize my _____ above all else.

_____

_____

Tuesday. My name is _____ and I am a _____.
I do not _____ *no matter what.* I prioritize my _____ above all else.

_____

_____

Wednesday. My name is _____ and I am a _____.
I do not _____ *no matter what.* I prioritize my _____ above all else.

_____

_____

Thursday. My name is _____ and I am a _____.
I do not _____ *no matter what.* I prioritize my _____ above all else.

_____

_____

Friday. My name is _____ and I am a _____.
I do not _____ *no matter what.* I prioritize my _____ above all else.

_____

_____

Saturday. My name is _____ and I am a _____.
I do not _____ *no matter what.* I prioritize my _____ above all else.

_____

_____

Congratulations! You have achieved your fourth week of sobriety!

WEEK 5: __/__/__ to __/__/__

I slept last night—I did not pass out. Today I will not drink, and tonight I will sleep again.

Sunday. My name is _____ and I am a _____.
I do not _____ *no matter what.* I prioritize my _____ above all else.
_____
_____

Monday. My name is _____ and I am a _____.
I do not _____ *no matter what.* I prioritize my _____ above all else.
_____
_____

Tuesday. My name is _____ and I am a _____.
I do not _____ *no matter what.* I prioritize my _____ above all else.
_____
_____

Wednesday. My name is _____ and I am a _____.
I do not _____ *no matter what.* I prioritize my _____ above all else.
_____
_____

Thursday. My name is _____ and I am a _____.
I do not _____ *no matter what.* I prioritize my _____ above all else.
_____
_____

Friday. My name is _____ and I am a _____.
I do not _____ *no matter what.* I prioritize my _____ above all else.
_____
_____

Saturday. My name is _____ and I am a _____.
I do not _____ *no matter what.* I prioritize my _____ above all else.
_____
_____

Congratulations! You have achieved your fifth week of sobriety!

WEEK 6: __/__/__ to __/__/__

I will not drink today. My sobriety protects me from the grip of alcoholism.

Sunday. My name is _____ and I am a _____.
I do not _____ *no matter what.* I prioritize my _____ above all else.

_____

_____

Monday. My name is _____ and I am a _____.
I do not _____ *no matter what.* I prioritize my _____ above all else.

_____

_____

Tuesday. My name is _____ and I am a _____.
I do not _____ *no matter what.* I prioritize my _____ above all else.

_____

_____

Wednesday. My name is _____ and I am a _____.
I do not _____ *no matter what.* I prioritize my _____ above all else.

_____

_____

Thursday. My name is _____ and I am a _____.
I do not _____ *no matter what.* I prioritize my _____ above all else.

_____

_____

Friday. My name is _____ and I am a _____.
I do not _____ *no matter what.* I prioritize my _____ above all else.

_____

_____

Saturday. My name is _____ and I am a _____.
I do not _____ *no matter what.* I prioritize my _____ above all else.

_____

_____

Congratulations! You have achieved your sixth week of sobriety!

WEEK 7: __/__/__ to __/__/__

I congratulate myself on every day of sobriety.

Sunday. My name is _____ and I am a _____.
I do not _____ *no matter what.* I prioritize my _____ above all else.

_____

_____

Monday. My name is _____ and I am a _____.
I do not _____ *no matter what.* I prioritize my _____ above all else.

_____

_____

Tuesday. My name is _____ and I am a _____.
I do not _____ *no matter what.* I prioritize my _____ above all else.

_____

_____

Wednesday. My name is _____ and I am a _____.
I do not _____ *no matter what.* I prioritize my _____ above all else.

_____

_____

Thursday. My name is _____ and I am a _____.
I do not _____ *no matter what.* I prioritize my _____ above all else.

_____

_____

Friday. My name is _____ and I am a _____.
I do not _____ *no matter what.* I prioritize my _____ above all else.

_____

_____

Saturday. My name is _____ and I am a _____.
I do not _____ *no matter what.* I prioritize my _____ above all else.

_____

_____

Congratulations! You have achieved your seventh week of sobriety!

WEEK 8: __/__/__ to __/__/__

I save my life each day by choosing not to drink.

Sunday. My name is _____ and I am a _____.
I do not _____ *no matter what*. I prioritize my _____ above all else.

_____

_____

Monday. My name is _____ and I am a _____.
I do not _____ *no matter what*. I prioritize my _____ above all else.

_____

_____

Tuesday. My name is _____ and I am a _____.
I do not _____ *no matter what*. I prioritize my _____ above all else.

_____

_____

Wednesday. My name is _____ and I am a _____.
I do not _____ *no matter what*. I prioritize my _____ above all else.

_____

_____

Thursday. My name is _____ and I am a _____.
I do not _____ *no matter what*. I prioritize my _____ above all else.

_____

_____

Friday. My name is _____ and I am a _____.
I do not _____ *no matter what*. I prioritize my _____ above all else.

_____

_____

Saturday. My name is _____ and I am a _____.
I do not _____ *no matter what*. I prioritize my _____ above all else.

_____

_____

Congratulations! You have achieved your eighth week of sobriety!

WEEK 9: __/__/__ to __/__/__

No matter what happens, I just won't drink today.

Sunday. My name is _____ and I am a _____.
I do not _____ *no matter what.* I prioritize my _____ above all else.

_____

_____

Monday. My name is _____ and I am a _____.
I do not _____ *no matter what.* I prioritize my _____ above all else.

_____

_____

Tuesday. My name is _____ and I am a _____.
I do not _____ *no matter what.* I prioritize my _____ above all else.

_____

_____

Wednesday. My name is _____ and I am a _____.
I do not _____ *no matter what.* I prioritize my _____ above all else.

_____

_____

Thursday. My name is _____ and I am a _____.
I do not _____ *no matter what.* I prioritize my _____ above all else.

_____

_____

Friday. My name is _____ and I am a _____.
I do not _____ *no matter what.* I prioritize my _____ above all else.

_____

_____

Saturday. My name is _____ and I am a _____.
I do not _____ *no matter what.* I prioritize my _____ above all else.

_____

_____

Congratulations! You have achieved your ninth week of sobriety!

WEEK 10: __/__/__ to __/__/__

I choose sobriety today. Alcohol never fixed anything for me.

Sunday. My name is _____ and I am a _____.
I do not _____ *no matter what.* I prioritize my _____ above all else.

_____

_____

Monday. My name is _____ and I am a _____.
I do not _____ *no matter what.* I prioritize my _____ above all else.

_____

_____

Tuesday. My name is _____ and I am a _____.
I do not _____ *no matter what.* I prioritize my _____ above all else.

_____

_____

Wednesday. My name is _____ and I am a _____.
I do not _____ *no matter what.* I prioritize my _____ above all else.

_____

_____

Thursday. My name is _____ and I am a _____.
I do not _____ *no matter what.* I prioritize my _____ above all else.

_____

_____

Friday. My name is _____ and I am a _____.
I do not _____ *no matter what.* I prioritize my _____ above all else.

_____

_____

Saturday. My name is _____ and I am a _____.
I do not _____ *no matter what.* I prioritize my _____ above all else.

_____

_____

Congratulations! You have achieved your tenth week of sobriety!

WEEK 11: __/__/__ to __/__/__

I will avoid the horrors of active alcoholism by staying sober today.

Sunday. My name is _____ and I am a _____.
I do not _____ *no matter what.* I prioritize my _____ above all else.

_____

_____

Monday. My name is _____ and I am a _____.
I do not _____ *no matter what.* I prioritize my _____ above all else.

_____

Tuesday. My name is _____ and I am a _____.
I do not _____ *no matter what.* I prioritize my _____ above all else.

_____

_____

Wednesday. My name is _____ and I am a _____.
I do not _____ *no matter what.* I prioritize my _____ above all else.

_____

Thursday. My name is _____ and I am a _____.
I do not _____ *no matter what.* I prioritize my _____ above all else.

_____

_____

Friday. My name is _____ and I am a _____.
I do not _____ *no matter what.* I prioritize my _____ above all else.

_____

Saturday. My name is _____ and I am a _____.
I do not _____ *no matter what.* I prioritize my _____ above all else.

_____

_____

Congratulations! You have achieved your eleventh week of sobriety!

WEEK 12: __/__/__ to __/__/__

I will escape the demands of my addiction by staying sober today.

Sunday. My name is _____ and I am a _____.
I do not _____ *no matter what.* I prioritize my _____ above all else.

_____

_____

Monday. My name is _____ and I am a _____.
I do not _____ *no matter what.* I prioritize my _____ above all else.

_____

_____

Tuesday. My name is _____ and I am a _____.
I do not _____ *no matter what.* I prioritize my _____ above all else.

_____

_____

Wednesday. My name is _____ and I am a _____.
I do not _____ *no matter what.* I prioritize my _____ above all else.

_____

_____

Thursday. My name is _____ and I am a _____.
I do not _____ *no matter what.* I prioritize my _____ above all else.

_____

_____

Friday. My name is _____ and I am a _____.
I do not _____ *no matter what.* I prioritize my _____ above all else.

_____

_____

Saturday. My name is _____ and I am a _____.
I do not _____ *no matter what.* I prioritize my _____ above all else.

_____

_____

Congratulations! You have achieved your twelfth week of sobriety!

WEEK 13: __/__/__ to __/__/__

Sounds are no longer unbearable. In sobriety, I can tolerate what I never could while suffering constant hangovers.

Sunday. My name is _____ and I am a _____.
I do not _____ *no matter what.* I prioritize my _____ above all else.

_____

_____

Monday. My name is _____ and I am a _____.
I do not _____ *no matter what.* I prioritize my _____ above all else.

_____

_____

Tuesday. My name is _____ and I am a _____.
I do not _____ *no matter what.* I prioritize my _____ above all else.

_____

_____

Wednesday. My name is _____ and I am a _____.
I do not _____ *no matter what.* I prioritize my _____ above all else.

_____

_____

Thursday. My name is _____ and I am a _____.
I do not _____ *no matter what.* I prioritize my _____ above all else.

_____

_____

Friday. My name is _____ and I am a _____.
I do not _____ *no matter what.* I prioritize my _____ above all else.

_____

_____

Saturday. My name is _____ and I am a _____.
I do not _____ *no matter what.* I prioritize my _____ above all else.

_____

_____

Congratulations! You have achieved your thirteenth week of sobriety!

WEEK 14: __/__/__ to __/__/__

I choose sobriety today; thus I triumph over alcohol.

Sunday. My name is _____ and I am a _____.
I do not _____ *no matter what.* I prioritize my _____ above all else.

Monday. My name is _____ and I am a _____.
I do not _____ *no matter what.* I prioritize my _____ above all else.

Tuesday. My name is _____ and I am a _____.
I do not _____ *no matter what.* I prioritize my _____ above all else.

Wednesday. My name is _____ and I am a _____.
I do not _____ *no matter what.* I prioritize my _____ above all else.

Thursday. My name is _____ and I am a _____.
I do not _____ *no matter what.* I prioritize my _____ above all else.

Friday. My name is _____ and I am a _____.
I do not _____ *no matter what.* I prioritize my _____ above all else.

Saturday. My name is _____ and I am a _____.
I do not _____ *no matter what.* I prioritize my _____ above all else.

Congratulations! You have achieved your fourteenth week of sobriety!

WEEK 15: __/__/__ to __/__/__

I have a real life today. I have my sobriety.

Sunday. My name is _____ and I am a _____.
I do not _____ *no matter what.* I prioritize my _____ above all else.

Monday. My name is _____ and I am a _____.
I do not _____ *no matter what.* I prioritize my _____ above all else.

Tuesday. My name is _____ and I am a _____.
I do not _____ *no matter what.* I prioritize my _____ above all else.

Wednesday. My name is _____ and I am a _____.
I do not _____ *no matter what.* I prioritize my _____ above all else.

Thursday. My name is _____ and I am a _____.
I do not _____ *no matter what.* I prioritize my _____ above all else.

Friday. My name is _____ and I am a _____.
I do not _____ *no matter what.* I prioritize my _____ above all else.

Saturday. My name is _____ and I am a _____.
I do not _____ *no matter what.* I prioritize my _____ above all else.

Congratulations! You have achieved your fifteenth week of sobriety!

WEEK 16: __/__/__ to __/__/__

The sky seems bluer when I am sober. The birds sing, and now I am actually aware of their singing.

Sunday. My name is _____ and I am a _____.
I do not _____ *no matter what.* I prioritize my _____ above all else.

_____

_____

Monday. My name is _____ and I am a _____.
I do not _____ *no matter what.* I prioritize my _____ above all else.

_____

_____

Tuesday. My name is _____ and I am a _____.
I do not _____ *no matter what.* I prioritize my _____ above all else.

_____

_____

Wednesday. My name is _____ and I am a _____.
I do not _____ *no matter what.* I prioritize my _____ above all else.

_____

_____

Thursday. My name is _____ and I am a _____.
I do not _____ *no matter what.* I prioritize my _____ above all else.

_____

_____

Friday. My name is _____ and I am a _____.
I do not _____ *no matter what.* I prioritize my _____ above all else.

_____

_____

Saturday. My name is _____ and I am a _____.
I do not _____ *no matter what.* I prioritize my _____ above all else.

_____

_____

Congratulations! You have achieved your sixteenth week of sobriety!

WEEK 17: __/__/__ to __/__/__

I need time to heal, both physically and emotionally. It is painful, but drinking is more painful.

Sunday. My name is _____ and I am a _____.
I do not _____ *no matter what.* I prioritize my _____ above all else

_____

_____

Monday. My name is _____ and I am a _____.
I do not _____ *no matter what.* I prioritize my _____ above all else.

_____

_____

Tuesday. My name is _____ and I am a _____.
I do not _____ *no matter what.* I prioritize my _____ above all else.

_____

_____

Wednesday. My name is _____ and I am a _____.
I do not _____ *no matter what.* I prioritize my _____ above all else

_____

_____

Thursday. My name is _____ and I am a _____.
I do not _____ *no matter what.* I prioritize my _____ above all else.

_____

_____

Friday. My name is _____ and I am a _____.
I do not _____ *no matter what.* I prioritize my _____ above all else

_____

_____

Saturday. My name is _____ and I am a _____.
I do not _____ *no matter what.* I prioritize my _____ above all else.

_____

_____

Congratulations! You have achieved your seventeenth week of sobriety!

WEEK 18: __/__/__ to __/__/__

Today I have hope as I choose sobriety, one day at a time.

Sunday. My name is _____ and I am a _____.
I do not _____ *no matter what.* I prioritize my _____ above all else.

_____

_____

Monday. My name is _____ and I am a _____.
I do not _____ *no matter what.* I prioritize my _____ above all else.

_____

_____

Tuesday. My name is _____ and I am a _____.
I do not _____ *no matter what.* I prioritize my _____ above all else.

_____

_____

Wednesday. My name is _____ and I am a _____.
I do not _____ *no matter what.* I prioritize my _____ above all else.

_____

_____

Thursday. My name is _____ and I am a _____.
I do not _____ *no matter what.* I prioritize my _____ above all else.

_____

_____

Friday. My name is _____ and I am a _____.
I do not _____ *no matter what.* I prioritize my _____ above all else.

_____

_____

Saturday. My name is _____ and I am a _____.
I do not _____ *no matter what.* I prioritize my _____ above all else.

_____

_____

Congratulations! You have achieved your eighteenth week of sobriety!

WEEK 19: __/__/__ to __/__/__

Whether I'm feeling good or bad, I still have the achievement of sobriety.

Sunday. My name is _____ and I am a _____.
I do not _____ *no matter what.* I prioritize my _____ above all else.

_____

_____

Monday. My name is _____ and I am a _____.
I do not _____ *no matter what.* I prioritize my _____ above all else.

_____

_____

Tuesday. My name is _____ and I am a _____.
I do not _____ *no matter what.* I prioritize my _____ above all else.

_____

_____

Wednesday. My name is _____ and I am a _____.
I do not _____ *no matter what.* I prioritize my _____ above all else.

_____

_____

Thursday. My name is _____ and I am a _____.
I do not _____ *no matter what.* I prioritize my _____ above all else.

_____

_____

Friday. My name is _____ and I am a _____.
I do not _____ *no matter what.* I prioritize my _____ above all else.

_____

_____

Saturday. My name is _____ and I am a _____.
I do not _____ *no matter what.* I prioritize my _____ above all else.

_____

_____

Congratulations! You have achieved your nineteenth week of sobriety!

WEEK 20: __/__/__ to __/__/__

The simplest pleasures are fulfilling to me in sobriety, and that makes me feel good.

Sunday. My name is _____ and I am a _____.
I do not _____ *no matter what.* I prioritize my _____ above all else.

_____

_____

Monday. My name is _____ and I am a _____.
I do not _____ *no matter what.* I prioritize my _____ above all else.

_____

_____

Tuesday. My name is _____ and I am a _____.
I do not _____ *no matter what.* I prioritize my _____ above all else.

_____

_____

Wednesday. My name is _____ and I am a _____.
I do not _____ *no matter what.* I prioritize my _____ above all else.

_____

_____

Thursday. My name is _____ and I am a _____.
I do not _____ *no matter what.* I prioritize my _____ above all else.

_____

_____

Friday. My name is _____ and I am a _____.
I do not _____ *no matter what.* I prioritize my _____ above all else.

_____

_____

Saturday. My name is _____ and I am a _____.
I do not _____ *no matter what.* I prioritize my _____ above all else.

_____

_____

Congratulations! You have achieved your twentieth week of sobriety!

WEEK 21: __/__/__ to __/__/__

Even when I have problems, I am sober; the down side is not so steep, nor is it razor sharp.

Sunday. My name is _____ and I am a _____.
I do not _____ *no matter what.* I prioritize my _____ above all else.

_____

_____

Monday. My name is _____ and I am a _____.
I do not _____ *no matter what.* I prioritize my _____ above all else.

_____

_____

Tuesday. My name is _____ and I am a _____.
I do not _____ *no matter what.* I prioritize my _____ above all else.

_____

_____

Wednesday. My name is _____ and I am a _____.
I do not _____ *no matter what.* I prioritize my _____ above all else.

_____

_____

Thursday. My name is _____ and I am a _____.
I do not _____ *no matter what.* I prioritize my _____ above all else.

_____

_____

Friday. My name is _____ and I am a _____.
I do not _____ *no matter what.* I prioritize my _____ above all else.

_____

_____

Saturday. My name is _____ and I am a _____.
I do not _____ *no matter what.* I prioritize my _____ above all else.

_____

_____

Congratulations! You have achieved your twenty-first week of sobriety!

WEEK 22: __/__/__ to __/__/__

Even television is better in sobriety. I no longer view the test pattern in earnest.

Sunday. My name is _____ and I am a _____.
I do not _____ *no matter what.* I prioritize my _____ above all else.

_____

_____

Monday. My name is _____ and I am a _____.
I do not _____ *no matter what.* I prioritize my _____ above all else.

_____

_____

Tuesday. My name is _____ and I am a _____.
I do not _____ *no matter what.* I prioritize my _____ above all else.

_____

_____

Wednesday. My name is _____ and I am a _____.
I do not _____ *no matter what.* I prioritize my _____ above all else.

_____

_____

Thursday. My name is _____ and I am a _____.
I do not _____ *no matter what.* I prioritize my _____ above all else.

_____

_____

Friday. My name is _____ and I am a _____.
I do not _____ *no matter what.* I prioritize my _____ above all else.

_____

_____

Saturday. My name is _____ and I am a _____.
I do not _____ *no matter what.* I prioritize my _____ above all else.

_____

_____

Congratulations! You have achieved your twenty-second week of sobriety!

WEEK 23: __/__/__ to __/__/__

I can do so much more today than I could when I was drinking. My sobriety affords me this.

Sunday. My name is _____ and I am a _____.
I do not _____ *no matter what.* I prioritize my _____ above all else.

_____

_____

Monday. My name is _____ and I am a _____.
I do not _____ *no matter what.* I prioritize my _____ above all else.

_____

_____

Tuesday. My name is _____ and I am a _____.
I do not _____ *no matter what.* I prioritize my _____ above all else.

_____

_____

Wednesday. My name is _____ and I am a _____.
I do not _____ *no matter what.* I prioritize my _____ above all else.

_____

_____

Thursday. My name is _____ and I am a _____.
I do not _____ *no matter what.* I prioritize my _____ above all else.

_____

_____

Friday. My name is _____ and I am a _____.
I do not _____ *no matter what.* I prioritize my _____ above all else.

_____

_____

Saturday. My name is _____ and I am a _____.
I do not _____ *no matter what.* I prioritize my _____ above all else.

_____

_____

Congratulations! You have achieved your twenty-third week of sobriety!

WEEK 24: __/__/__ to __/__/__

My mirror is no longer my enemy. I may not be Prince Charming or Miss America, but I see an honest face peering back at me in sobriety.

Sunday. My name is _____ and I am a _____.
I do not _____ *no matter what.* I prioritize my _____ above all else.

_____

_____

Monday. My name is _____ and I am a _____.
I do not _____ *no matter what.* I prioritize my _____ above all else.

_____

_____

Tuesday. My name is _____ and I am a _____.
I do not _____ *no matter what.* I prioritize my _____ above all else.

_____

_____

Wednesday. My name is _____ and I am a _____.
I do not _____ *no matter what.* I prioritize my _____ above all else.

_____

_____

Thursday. My name is _____ and I am a _____.
I do not _____ *no matter what.* I prioritize my _____ above all else.

_____

_____

Friday. My name is _____ and I am a _____.
I do not _____ *no matter what.* I prioritize my _____ above all else.

_____

_____

Saturday. My name is _____ and I am a _____.
I do not _____ *no matter what.* I prioritize my _____ above all else.

_____

_____

Congratulations! You have achieved your twenty-fourth week of sobriety!

WEEK 25: __/__/__ to __/__/__

Brisk walks or leisurely strolls make me feel good and, being sober, I am now able to enjoy them safely.

Sunday. My name is _____ and I am a _____.
I do not _____ *no matter what.* I prioritize my _____ above all else.

_____

_____

Monday. My name is _____ and I am a _____.
I do not _____ *no matter what.* I prioritize my _____ above all else.

_____

_____

Tuesday. My name is _____ and I am a _____.
I do not _____ *no matter what.* I prioritize my _____ above all else.

_____

_____

Wednesday. My name is _____ and I am a _____.
I do not _____ *no matter what.* I prioritize my _____ above all else.

_____

_____

Thursday. My name is _____ and I am a _____.
I do not _____ *no matter what.* I prioritize my _____ above all else.

_____

_____

Friday. My name is _____ and I am a _____.
I do not _____ *no matter what.* I prioritize my _____ above all else.

_____

_____

Saturday. My name is _____ and I am a _____.
I do not _____ *no matter what.* I prioritize my _____ above all else.

_____

_____

Congratulations! You have achieved your twenty-fifth week of sobriety!

WEEK 26: __/__/__ to __/__/__

Molehills remain molehills today. In sobriety I am less likely to view them as mountains.

Sunday. My name is _____ and I am a _____.
I do not _____ *no matter what.* I prioritize my _____ above all else.

_____

_____

Monday. My name is _____ and I am a _____.
I do not _____ *no matter what.* I prioritize my _____ above all else.

_____

_____

Tuesday. My name is _____ and I am a _____.
I do not _____ *no matter what.* I prioritize my _____ above all else.

_____

_____

Wednesday. My name is _____ and I am a _____.
I do not _____ *no matter what.* I prioritize my _____ above all else.

_____

_____

Thursday. My name is _____ and I am a _____.
I do not _____ *no matter what.* I prioritize my _____ above all else.

_____

_____

Friday. My name is _____ and I am a _____.
I do not _____ *no matter what.* I prioritize my _____ above all else.

_____

_____

Saturday. My name is _____ and I am a _____.
I do not _____ *no matter what.* I prioritize my _____ above all else.

_____

_____

Congratulations! You have achieved your twenty-sixth week of sobriety!

WEEK 27: __/__/__ to __/__/__

I am the guardian of my sobriety, and this sets me free, one day at a time.

Sunday. My name is _____ and I am a _____.
I do not _____ *no matter what.* I prioritize my _____ above all else.

_____

_____

Monday. My name is _____ and I am a _____.
I do not _____ *no matter what.* I prioritize my _____ above all else.

_____

_____

Tuesday. My name is _____ and I am a _____.
I do not _____ *no matter what.* I prioritize my _____ above all else.

_____

_____

Wednesday. My name is _____ and I am a _____.
I do not _____ *no matter what.* I prioritize my _____ above all else.

_____

_____

Thursday. My name is _____ and I am a _____.
I do not _____ *no matter what.* I prioritize my _____ above all else.

_____

_____

Friday. My name is _____ and I am a _____.
I do not _____ *no matter what.* I prioritize my _____ above all else.

_____

_____

Saturday. My name is _____ and I am a _____.
I do not _____ *no matter what.* I prioritize my _____ above all else.

_____

_____

Congratulations! You have achieved your twenty-seventh week of sobriety!

WEEK 28: ___/___/___ to ___/___/___

In sobriety I have the ability to learn, to reason, and to grow.

Sunday. My name is _____ and I am a _____.
I do not _____ *no matter what.* I prioritize my _____ above all else.

_____

_____

Monday. My name is _____ and I am a _____.
I do not _____ *no matter what.* I prioritize my _____ above all else.

_____

_____

Tuesday. My name is _____ and I am a _____.
I do not _____ *no matter what.* I prioritize my _____ above all else.

_____

_____

Wednesday. My name is _____ and I am a _____.
I do not _____ *no matter what.* I prioritize my _____ above all else.

_____

_____

Thursday. My name is _____ and I am a _____.
I do not _____ *no matter what.* I prioritize my _____ above all else.

_____

_____

Friday. My name is _____ and I am a _____.
I do not _____ *no matter what.* I prioritize my _____ above all else.

_____

_____

Saturday. My name is _____ and I am a _____.
I do not _____ *no matter what.* I prioritize my _____ above all else.

_____

_____

Congratulations! You have achieved your twenty-eighth week of sobriety!

WEEK 29: __/__/__ to __/__/__

I no longer babble incoherently, thinking I am clever. In sobriety my thoughts and words are clearer.

Sunday. My name is _____ and I am a _____.
I do not _____ *no matter what.* I prioritize my _____ above all else.

_____

_____

Monday. My name is _____ and I am a _____.
I do not _____ *no matter what.* I prioritize my _____ above all else.

_____

_____

Tuesday. My name is _____ and I am a _____.
I do not _____ *no matter what.* I prioritize my _____ above all else.

_____

_____

Wednesday. My name is _____ and I am a _____.
I do not _____ *no matter what.* I prioritize my _____ above all else.

_____

_____

Thursday. My name is _____ and I am a _____.
I do not _____ *no matter what.* I prioritize my _____ above all else.

_____

_____

Friday. My name is _____ and I am a _____.
I do not _____ *no matter what.* I prioritize my _____ above all else.

_____

_____

Saturday. My name is _____ and I am a _____.
I do not _____ *no matter what.* I prioritize my _____ above all else.

_____

_____

Congratulations! You have achieved your twenty-ninth week of sobriety!

WEEK 30: __/__/__ to __/__/__

In sobriety it is possible for me to reach out to others.

Sunday. My name is _____ and I am a _____.
I do not _____ *no matter what.* I prioritize my _____ above all else.

_____

_____

Monday. My name is _____ and I am a _____.
I do not _____ *no matter what.* I prioritize my _____ above all else.

_____

_____

Tuesday. My name is _____ and I am a _____.
I do not _____ *no matter what.* I prioritize my _____ above all else.

_____

_____

Wednesday. My name is _____ and I am a _____.
I do not _____ *no matter what.* I prioritize my _____ above all else.

_____

_____

Thursday. My name is _____ and I am a _____.
I do not _____ *no matter what.* I prioritize my _____ above all else.

_____

_____

Friday. My name is _____ and I am a _____.
I do not _____ *no matter what.* I prioritize my _____ above all else.

_____

_____

Saturday. My name is _____ and I am a _____.
I do not _____ *no matter what.* I prioritize my _____ above all else.

_____

_____

Congratulations! You have achieved your thirtieth week of sobriety!

WEEK 31: __/__/__ to __/__/__

When I travel in sobriety, I know where I'm going and where I've been.

Sunday. My name is _____ and I am a _____.
I do not _____ *no matter what.* I prioritize my _____ above all else.

_____

_____

Monday. My name is _____ and I am a _____.
I do not _____ *no matter what.* I prioritize my _____ above all else.

_____

_____

Tuesday. My name is _____ and I am a _____.
I do not _____ *no matter what.* I prioritize my _____ above all else.

_____

_____

Wednesday. My name is _____ and I am a _____.
I do not _____ *no matter what.* I prioritize my _____ above all else.

_____

_____

Thursday. My name is _____ and I am a _____.
I do not _____ *no matter what.* I prioritize my _____ above all else.

_____

_____

Friday. My name is _____ and I am a _____.
I do not _____ *no matter what.* I prioritize my _____ above all else.

_____

_____

Saturday. My name is _____ and I am a _____.
I do not _____ *no matter what.* I prioritize my _____ above all else.

_____

_____

Congratulations! You have achieved your thirty-first week of sobriety!

WEEK 32: __/__/__ to __/__/__

I have the opportunity to keep commitments today, to myself and to others.

Sunday. My name is _____ and I am a _____.
I do not _____ *no matter what.* I prioritize my _____ above all else.

_____

_____

Monday. My name is _____ and I am a _____.
I do not _____ *no matter what.* I prioritize my _____ above all else.

_____

_____

Tuesday. My name is _____ and I am a _____.
I do not _____ *no matter what.* I prioritize my _____ above all else.

_____

_____

Wednesday. My name is _____ and I am a _____.
I do not _____ *no matter what.* I prioritize my _____ above all else.

_____

_____

Thursday. My name is _____ and I am a _____.
I do not _____ *no matter what.* I prioritize my _____ above all else.

_____

_____

Friday. My name is _____ and I am a _____.
I do not _____ *no matter what.* I prioritize my _____ above all else.

_____

_____

Saturday. My name is _____ and I am a _____.
I do not _____ *no matter what.* I prioritize my _____ above all else.

_____

_____

Congratulations! You have achieved your thirty-second week of sobriety!

WEEK 33: __/__/__ to __/__/__

Silence is golden today. In sobriety, I no longer hear my cries of despair. I have hope.

Sunday. My name is _____ and I am a _____.
I do not _____ *no matter what.* I prioritize my _____ above all else

_____

_____

Monday. My name is _____ and I am a _____.
I do not _____ *no matter what.* I prioritize my _____ above all else

_____

_____

Tuesday. My name is _____ and I am a _____
I do not _____ *no matter what.* I prioritize my _____ above all else

_____

_____

Wednesday. My name is _____ and I am a _____
I do not _____ *no matter what.* I prioritize my _____ above all else.

_____

_____

Thursday. My name is _____ and I am a _____
I do not _____ *no matter what.* I prioritize my _____ above all else

_____

_____

Friday. My name is _____ and I am a _____.
I do not _____ *no matter what.* I prioritize my _____ above all else.

_____

_____

Saturday. My name is _____ and I am a _____.
I do not _____ *no matter what.* I prioritize my _____ above all else.

_____

_____

Congratulations! You have achieved your thirty-third week of sobriety!

WEEK 34: __/__/__ to __/__/__

I didn't wake up in a strange bed today. I chose where and with whom I slept last night.

Sunday. My name is _____ and I am a _____.
I do not _____ *no matter what.* I prioritize my _____ above all else.

_____

_____

Monday. My name is _____ and I am a _____.
I do not _____ *no matter what.* I prioritize my _____ above all else.

_____

_____

Tuesday. My name is _____ and I am a _____.
I do not _____ *no matter what.* I prioritize my _____ above all else.

_____

_____

Wednesday. My name is _____ and I am a _____.
I do not _____ *no matter what.* I prioritize my _____ above all else.

_____

_____

Thursday. My name is _____ and I am a _____.
I do not _____ *no matter what.* I prioritize my _____ above all else.

_____

_____

Friday. My name is _____ and I am a _____.
I do not _____ *no matter what.* I prioritize my _____ above all else.

_____

_____

Saturday. My name is _____ and I am a _____.
I do not _____ *no matter what.* I prioritize my _____ above all else.

_____

_____

Congratulations! You have achieved your thirty-fourth week of sobriety!

WEEK 35: __/__/__ to __/__/__

I don't have to make lame excuses to my family, friends, or employer today. I am sober.

Sunday. My name is _____ and I am a _____.
I do not _____ *no matter what.* I prioritize my _____ above all else.

_____

_____

Monday. My name is _____ and I am a _____.
I do not _____ *no matter what.* I prioritize my _____ above all else.

_____

_____

Tuesday. My name is _____ and I am a _____.
I do not _____ *no matter what.* I prioritize my _____ above all else

_____

_____

Wednesday. My name is _____ and I am a _____.
I do not _____ *no matter what.* I prioritize my _____ above all else.

_____

_____

Thursday. My name is _____ and I am a _____.
I do not _____ *no matter what.* I prioritize my _____ above all else.

_____

_____

Friday. My name is _____ and I am a _____.
I do not _____ *no matter what.* I prioritize my _____ above all else.

_____

_____

Saturday. My name is _____ and I am a _____.
I do not _____ *no matter what.* I prioritize my _____ above all else.

_____

_____

Congratulations! You have achieved your thirty-fifth week of sobriety!

WEEK 36: __/__/__ to __/__/__

I'm aware of the calls on my phone bill today. I have avoided "blackout dialing fever" by choosing sobriety.

Sunday. My name is _____ and I am a _____.
I do not _____ *no matter what.* I prioritize my _____ above all else.

_____

_____

Monday. My name is _____ and I am a _____.
I do not _____ *no matter what.* I prioritize my _____ above all else.

_____

_____

Tuesday. My name is _____ and I am a _____.
I do not _____ *no matter what.* I prioritize my _____ above all else.

_____

_____

Wednesday. My name is _____ and I am a _____.
I do not _____ *no matter what.* I prioritize my _____ above all else.

_____

_____

Thursday. My name is _____ and I am a _____.
I do not _____ *no matter what.* I prioritize my _____ above all else.

_____

_____

Friday. My name is _____ and I am a _____.
I do not _____ *no matter what.* I prioritize my _____ above all else.

_____

_____

Saturday. My name is _____ and I am a _____.
I do not _____ *no matter what.* I prioritize my _____ above all else.

_____

_____

Congratulations! You have achieved your thirty-sixth week of sobriety!

WEEK 37: __/__/__ to __/__/__

I don't have to wonder which apologies are owed to whom today. I am living sober now.

Sunday. My name is _____ and I am a _____.
I do not _____ *no matter what.* I prioritize my _____ above all else.

_____

_____

Monday. My name is _____ and I am a _____.
I do not _____ *no matter what.* I prioritize my _____ above all else.

_____

_____

Tuesday. My name is _____ and I am a _____.
I do not _____ *no matter what.* I prioritize my _____ above all else.

_____

_____

Wednesday. My name is _____ and I am a _____.
I do not _____ *no matter what.* I prioritize my _____ above all else.

_____

_____

Thursday. My name is _____ and I am a _____.
I do not _____ *no matter what.* I prioritize my _____ above all else.

_____

_____

Friday. My name is _____ and I am a _____.
I do not _____ *no matter what.* I prioritize my _____ above all else.

_____

_____

Saturday. My name is _____ and I am a _____.
I do not _____ *no matter what.* I prioritize my _____ above all else.

_____

_____

Congratulations! You have achieved your thirty-seventh week of sobriety!

WEEK 38: __/__/__ to __/__/__

I have the real ability to think and feel, and to act on these thoughts and feelings today. I had only illusions when drinking.

Sunday. My name is _____ and I am a _____.
I do not _____ *no matter what.* I prioritize my _____ above all else.

_____

_____

Monday. My name is _____ and I am a _____.
I do not _____ *no matter what.* I prioritize my _____ above all else.

_____

_____

Tuesday. My name is _____ and I am a _____.
I do not _____ *no matter what.* I prioritize my _____ above all else.

_____

_____

Wednesday. My name is _____ and I am a _____.
I do not _____ *no matter what.* I prioritize my _____ above all else.

_____

_____

Thursday. My name is _____ and I am a _____.
I do not _____ *no matter what.* I prioritize my _____ above all else.

_____

_____

Friday. My name is _____ and I am a _____.
I do not _____ *no matter what.* I prioritize my _____ above all else.

_____

_____

Saturday. My name is _____ and I am a _____.
I do not _____ *no matter what.* I prioritize my _____ above all else.

_____

_____

Congratulations! You have achieved your thirty-eighth week of sobriety!

WEEK 39: __/__/__ to __/__/__

My life today is more meaningful than my previous soap-opera existence, played out through a bottle.

Sunday. My name is _____ and I am a _____.
I do not _____ *no matter what.* I prioritize my _____ above all else.

Monday. My name is _____ and I am a _____.
I do not _____ *no matter what.* I prioritize my _____ above all else.

Tuesday. My name is _____ and I am a _____.
I do not _____ *no matter what.* I prioritize my _____ above all else.

Wednesday. My name is _____ and I am a _____.
I do not _____ *no matter what.* I prioritize my _____ above all else.

Thursday. My name is _____ and I am a _____.
I do not _____ *no matter what.* I prioritize my _____ above all else.

Friday. My name is _____ and I am a _____.
I do not _____ *no matter what.* I prioritize my _____ above all else.

Saturday. My name is _____ and I am a _____.
I do not _____ *no matter what.* I prioritize my _____ above all else.

Congratulations! You have achieved your thirty-ninth week of sobriety!

WEEK 40: __/__/__ to __/__/__

I have a right to my life today, and in sobriety, I have a life to claim.

Sunday. My name is _____ and I am a _____.
I do not _____ *no matter what.* I prioritize my _____ above all else.

_____

_____

Monday. My name is _____ and I am a _____.
I do not _____ *no matter what.* I prioritize my _____ above all else.

_____

_____

Tuesday. My name is _____ and I am a _____.
I do not _____ *no matter what.* I prioritize my _____ above all else.

_____

_____

Wednesday. My name is _____ and I am a _____.
I do not _____ *no matter what.* I prioritize my _____ above all else.

_____

_____

Thursday. My name is _____ and I am a _____.
I do not _____ *no matter what.* I prioritize my _____ above all else.

_____

_____

Friday. My name is _____ and I am a _____.
I do not _____ *no matter what.* I prioritize my _____ above all else.

_____

_____

Saturday. My name is _____ and I am a _____.
I do not _____ *no matter what.* I prioritize my _____ above all else.

_____

_____

Congratulations! You have achieved your fortieth week of sobriety!

WEEK 41: __/__/__ to __/__/__

Not every day is full of roses, but in sobriety, the thorns are fewer.

Sunday. My name is _____ and I am a _____.
I do not _____ *no matter what.* I prioritize my _____ above all else.

_____

_____

Monday. My name is _____ and I am a _____.
I do not _____ *no matter what.* I prioritize my _____ above all else.

_____

_____

Tuesday. My name is _____ and I am a _____.
I do not _____ *no matter what.* I prioritize my _____ above all else.

_____

_____

Wednesday. My name is _____ and I am a _____.
I do not _____ *no matter what.* I prioritize my _____ above all else.

_____

_____

Thursday. My name is _____ and I am a _____.
I do not _____ *no matter what.* I prioritize my _____ above all else.

_____

_____

Friday. My name is _____ and I am a _____.
I do not _____ *no matter what.* I prioritize my _____ above all else.

_____

_____

Saturday. My name is _____ and I am a _____.
I do not _____ *no matter what.* I prioritize my _____ above all else.

_____

_____

Congratulations! You have achieved your forty-first week of sobriety!

WEEK 42: __/__/__ to __/__/__

In sobriety I have the opportunity to take responsibility for my life. I an no longer a slave to alcohol.

Sunday. My name is _____ and I am a _____.
I do not _____ *no matter what.* I prioritize my _____ above all else.

_____

_____

Monday. My name is _____ and I am a _____.
I do not _____ *no matter what.* I prioritize my _____ above all else.

_____

_____

Tuesday. My name is _____ and I am a _____.
I do not _____ *no matter what.* I prioritize my _____ above all else.

_____

_____

Wednesday. My name is _____ and I am a _____.
I do not _____ *no matter what.* I prioritize my _____ above all else.

_____

_____

Thursday. My name is _____ and I am a _____.
I do not _____ *no matter what.* I prioritize my _____ above all else.

_____

_____

Friday. My name is _____ and I am a _____.
I do not _____ *no matter what.* I prioritize my _____ above all else.

_____

_____

Saturday. My name is _____ and I am a _____.
I do not _____ *no matter what.* I prioritize my _____ above all else.

_____

_____

Congratulations! You have achieved your forty-second week of sobriety!

WEEK 43: __/__/__ to __/__/__

Humankind has the propensity for rationality. By choosing sobriety, I protect my rational mind.

Sunday. My name is _____ and I am a _____.
I do not _____ *no matter what.* I prioritize my _____ above all else.

_____

_____

Monday. My name is _____ and I am a _____.
I do not _____ *no matter what.* I prioritize my _____ above all else.

_____

_____

Tuesday. My name is _____ and I am a _____.
I do not _____ *no matter what.* I prioritize my _____ above all else.

_____

_____

Wednesday. My name is _____ and I am a _____.
I do not _____ *no matter what.* I prioritize my _____ above all else.

_____

_____

Thursday. My name is _____ and I am a _____.
I do not _____ *no matter what.* I prioritize my _____ above all else.

_____

_____

Friday. My name is _____ and I am a _____.
I do not _____ *no matter what.* I prioritize my _____ above all else.

_____

_____

Saturday. My name is _____ and I am a _____.
I do not _____ *no matter what.* I prioritize my _____ above all else.

_____

_____

Congratulations! You have achieved your forty-third week of sobriety!

WEEK 44: __/__/__ to __/__/__

When opportunities come my way, at least I have a chance at them in sobriety.

Sunday. My name is _____ and I am a _____.
I do not _____ *no matter what.* I prioritize my _____ above all else.

_____

_____

Monday. My name is _____ and I am a _____.
I do not _____ *no matter what.* I prioritize my _____ above all else.

_____

_____

Tuesday. My name is _____ and I am a _____.
I do not _____ *no matter what.* I prioritize my _____ above all else.

_____

_____

Wednesday. My name is _____ and I am a _____.
I do not _____ *no matter what.* I prioritize my _____ above all else.

_____

_____

Thursday. My name is _____ and I am a _____.
I do not _____ *no matter what.* I prioritize my _____ above all else.

_____

_____

Friday. My name is _____ and I am a _____.
I do not _____ *no matter what.* I prioritize my _____ above all else.

_____

_____

Saturday. My name is _____ and I am a _____.
I do not _____ *no matter what.* I prioritize my _____ above all else.

_____

_____

Congratulations! You have achieved your forty-fourth week of sobriety!

WEEK 45: __/__/__ to __/__/__

Through my adventure of living sober, I gain awareness. This awareness and clarity grow one day at a time.

Sunday. My name is _____ and I am a _____.
I do not _____ *no matter what.* I prioritize my _____ above all else.

_____

_____

Monday. My name is _____ and I am a _____.
I do not _____ *no matter what.* I prioritize my _____ above all else.

_____

_____

Tuesday. My name is _____ and I am a _____.
I do not _____ *no matter what.* I prioritize my _____ above all else.

_____

_____

Wednesday. My name is _____ and I am a _____.
I do not _____ *no matter what.* I prioritize my _____ above all else.

_____

_____

Thursday. My name is _____ and I am a _____.
I do not _____ *no matter what.* I prioritize my _____ above all else.

_____

_____

Friday. My name is _____ and I am a _____.
I do not _____ *no matter what.* I prioritize my _____ above all else.

_____

_____

Saturday. My name is _____ and I am a _____.
I do not _____ *no matter what.* I prioritize my _____ above all else.

_____

_____

Congratulations! You have achieved your forty-fifth week of sobriety!

WEEK 46: __/__/__ to __/__/__

My sobriety allows me the opportunity to be creative today. What I thought was tortured creativity was really only torture.

Sunday. My name is _____ and I am a _____.
I do not _____ *no matter what.* I prioritize my _____ above all else.

_____

_____

Monday. My name is _____ and I am a _____.
I do not _____ *no matter what.* I prioritize my _____ above all else.

_____

_____

Tuesday. My name is _____ and I am a _____.
I do not _____ *no matter what.* I prioritize my _____ above all else.

_____

_____

Wednesday. My name is _____ and I am a _____.
I do not _____ *no matter what.* I prioritize my _____ above all else.

_____

_____

Thursday. My name is _____ and I am a _____.
I do not _____ *no matter what.* I prioritize my _____ above all else.

_____

_____

Friday. My name is _____ and I am a _____.
I do not _____ *no matter what.* I prioritize my _____ above all else.

_____

_____

Saturday. My name is _____ and I am a _____.
I do not _____ *no matter what.* I prioritize my _____ above all else.

_____

_____

Congratulations! You have achieved your forty-sixth week of sobriety!

WEEK 47: __/__/__ to __/__/__

I have a right to my life today, and in sobriety, I have a life to claim.

Sunday. My name is _____ and I am a _____.
I do not _____ *no matter what.* I prioritize my _____ above all else.

_____

_____

Monday. My name is _____ and I am a _____.
I do not _____ *no matter what.* I prioritize my _____ above all else.

_____

_____

Tuesday. My name is _____ and I am a _____.
I do not _____ *no matter what.* I prioritize my _____ above all else.

_____

_____

Wednesday. My name is _____ and I am a _____.
I do not _____ *no matter what.* I prioritize my _____ above all else.

_____

_____

Thursday. My name is _____ and I am a _____.
I do not _____ *no matter what.* I prioritize my _____ above all else.

_____

_____

Friday. My name is _____ and I am a _____.
I do not _____ *no matter what.* I prioritize my _____ above all else.

_____

_____

Saturday. My name is _____ and I am a _____.
I do not _____ *no matter what.* I prioritize my _____ above all else.

_____

_____

Congratulations! You have achieved your forty-seventh week of sobriety!

WEEK 48: __/__/__ to __/__/__

I have the opportunity to love today. I am sober.

Sunday. My name is _____ and I am a _____.
I do not _____ *no matter what*. I prioritize my _____ above all else.

_____

_____

Monday. My name is _____ and I am a _____.
I do not _____ *no matter what*. I prioritize my _____ above all else.

_____

_____

Tuesday. My name is _____ and I am a _____.
I do not _____ *no matter what*. I prioritize my _____ above all else.

_____

_____

Wednesday. My name is _____ and I am a _____.
I do not _____ *no matter what*. I prioritize my _____ above all else.

_____

_____

Thursday. My name is _____ and I am a _____.
I do not _____ *no matter what*. I prioritize my _____ above all else.

_____

_____

Friday. My name is _____ and I am a _____.
I do not _____ *no matter what*. I prioritize my _____ above all else.

_____

_____

Saturday. My name is _____ and I am a _____.
I do not _____ *no matter what*. I prioritize my _____ above all else.

_____

_____

Congratulations! You have achieved your forty-eighth week of sobriety!

WEEK 49: __/__/__ to __/__/__

My real feelings are no longer trapped in a bottle—in sobriety I can experience them fully.

Sunday. My name is _____ and I am a _____.
I do not _____ *no matter what.* I prioritize my _____ above all else.

_____

_____

Monday. My name is _____ and I am a _____.
I do not _____ *no matter what.* I prioritize my _____ above all else.

_____

_____

Tuesday. My name is _____ and I am a _____.
I do not _____ *no matter what.* I prioritize my _____ above all else.

_____

_____

Wednesday. My name is _____ and I am a _____.
I do not _____ *no matter what.* I prioritize my _____ above all else.

_____

_____

Thursday. My name is _____ and I am a _____.
I do not _____ *no matter what.* I prioritize my _____ above all else.

_____

_____

Friday. My name is _____ and I am a _____.
I do not _____ *no matter what.* I prioritize my _____ above all else.

_____

_____

Saturday. My name is _____ and I am a _____.
I do not _____ *no matter what.* I prioritize my _____ above all else.

_____

_____

Congratulations! You have achieved your forty-ninth week of sobriety!

WEEK 50: __/__/__ to __/__/__

My sobriety is one day at a time. I am building a bridge of life for myself, day after sober day.

Sunday. My name is _____ and I am a _____.
I do not _____ *no matter what.* I prioritize my _____ above all else.

_____

_____

Monday. My name is _____ and I am a _____.
I do not _____ *no matter what.* I prioritize my _____ above all else.

_____

_____

Tuesday. My name is _____ and I am a _____.
I do not _____ *no matter what.* I prioritize my _____ above all else.

_____

_____

Wednesday. My name is _____ and I am a _____.
I do not _____ *no matter what.* I prioritize my _____ above all else.

_____

_____

Thursday. My name is _____ and I am a _____.
I do not _____ *no matter what.* I prioritize my _____ above all else.

_____

_____

Friday. My name is _____ and I am a _____.
I do not _____ *no matter what.* I prioritize my _____ above all else.

_____

_____

Saturday. My name is _____ and I am a _____.
I do not _____ *no matter what.* I prioritize my _____ above all else.

_____

_____

Congratulations! You have achieved your fiftieth week of sobriety!

WEEK 51: __/__/__ to __/__/__

Sobriety allows me the strength of skepticism, rather than helplessness and gullibility. I am no longer an "easy mark."

Sunday. My name is _____ and I am a _____.
I do not _____ *no matter what.* I prioritize my _____ above all else.

_____

_____

Monday. My name is _____ and I am a _____.
I do not _____ *no matter what.* I prioritize my _____ above all else.

_____

_____

Tuesday. My name is _____ and I am a _____.
I do not _____ *no matter what.* I prioritize my _____ above all else.

_____

_____

Wednesday. My name is _____ and I am a _____.
I do not _____ *no matter what.* I prioritize my _____ above all else.

_____

_____

Thursday. My name is _____ and I am a _____.
I do not _____ *no matter what.* I prioritize my _____ above all else.

_____

_____

Friday. My name is _____ and I am a _____.
I do not _____ *no matter what.* I prioritize my _____ above all else.

_____

_____

Saturday. My name is _____ and I am a _____.
I do not _____ *no matter what.* I prioritize my _____ above all else.

_____

_____

Congratulations! You have achieved your fifty-first week of sobriety!

WEEK 52: __/__/__ to __/__/__

I am sober; therefore I am victorious today.

Sunday. My name is _____ and I am a _____.
I do not _____ *no matter what.* I prioritize my _____ above all else.

_____

_____

Monday. My name is _____ and I am a _____.
I do not _____ *no matter what.* I prioritize my _____ above all else.

_____

_____

Tuesday. My name is _____ and I am a _____.
I do not _____ *no matter what.* I prioritize my _____ above all else.

_____

_____

Wednesday. My name is _____ and I am a _____.
I do not _____ *no matter what.* I prioritize my _____ above all else.

_____

_____

Thursday. My name is _____ and I am a _____.
I do not _____ *no matter what.* I prioritize my _____ above all else.

_____

_____

Friday. My name is _____ and I am a _____.
I do not _____ *no matter what.* I prioritize my _____ above all else.

_____

_____

Saturday. My name is _____ and I am a _____.
I do not _____ *no matter what.* I prioritize my _____ above all else.

_____

_____

Congratulations on your first year of sobriety! Happy Birthday! *Your achievement is impressive!* You are now an inspiration to others. Continue to maintain your sobriety priority in good health and with all best wishes!

Appendix B
Press Releases

Usually newspapers prefer press releases to be as brief as possible, to the point, and double-spaced on 8½″ x 11″ letter-size white paper.

Because the publication may require additional information, the release and the envelope should list the address and phone number of a contact person. It is helpful if the contact person has a telephone answering machine or if the group rents a small post office box for inquiries. Direct press releases to the Editorial Department at newspapers and to the Program Director at radio and TV stations. Check your local telephone book's yellow pages for addresses. The same press release can be submitted as is to doctors, therapists, and Chemical Dependency Units in your community in order to make others aware of the existence of your alternative group.

FOR MORE INFORMATION   FOR IMMEDIATE
CONTACT: RELEASE
(*name*)   (*date*)
(*address*)
(*phone number*)

ALCOHOLICS STAYING SOBER
THROUGH SECULAR APPROACH

A new group for recovering alcoholics is now meeting on a regular basis in (*your area*). The Secular Sobriety Group (S.S.G.) is open to *all* alcoholics, especially to those who may be uncomfortable with the "Higher Power" religious concepts of other groups.

Alcoholics share with one another in an anonymous, informal, caring atmosphere. S.S.G. is nonprofit and there are no dues or fees. Weekly meetings are held on (*weeknight*) at (*time of meeting*) at (*name and street location of the facility you are using*). For information, please call (*name of contact person*) at (*area code and telephone number*).

— or —

STRATEGIES FOR SOBRIETY
OFFERED BY ALTERNATIVE GROUP

A new grassroots support group of recovering alcoholics is now holding informal meetings every _____ night at _____ P.M. in _____.

The thrust of these meetings is secular, rather than religious, offering an alternative for those who may be uncomfortable with the "Higher-Power" concepts of other groups.

The Secular Sobriety Group (S.S.G.) meets in the _____ facility located at _____ and offers a caring, candlelit atmosphere in which alcoholics can share their thoughts and feelings with one another on an anonymous basis.

Although the format for S.S.G. meetings is loosely structured, a recent topic, "Strategies For Staying Sober," evoked much interest and lively discussion.

This nonprofit grass-roots group is free and open to *all* alcoholics. For additional information call S.S.G. at _____.

— or —

SECULAR SOBRIETY GROUP:
ALTERNATIVE FOR ALCOHOLICS

An alternative grass-roots support group for recovering alcoholics is meeting each week. The Secular Sobriety Group (S.S.G.) appeals especially to persons who may be uncomfortable with "Higher-Power" concepts of more traditional, religious groups.

All alcoholics are welcome to attend at no charge on an anonymous basis. S.S.G. meets every _____ night at _____ P.M. in the _____ facility located at _____. For additional information phone S.S.G. at _____.

Appendix C
References

Under the Influence
A Guide to the Myths and Realities of Alcoholism
by Dr. James R. Milam and Katherine Ketcham
Bantam Books, Inc.
666 Fifth Avenue
New York, New York 10103

The Natural History of Alcoholism
Causes, Patterns, and Paths to Recovery
By Dr. George E. Vaillant
Harvard University Press
79 Garden Street
Cambridge, Massachusetts 02138

Free Inquiry
Published quarterly by the
Council for Democratic and Secular Humanism
Post Office Box 5
Buffalo, New York 14215

Prometheus Books
Free catalogue offers books on philosophy, ethics, science, humanism, free thought, education, social science, religion, the paranormal, and more.
700 East Amherst Street
Buffalo, New York 14215

Freethought Today
Published by the
Freedom from Religion Foundation
P.O. Box 750
Madison, Wisconsin 53701

Notes

CHAPTER 1

1. In *The Encyclopedia of Ignorance—Everything You Ever Wanted to Know About the Unknown,* edited by Ronald Duncan and Miranda Weston-Smith (New York: Pocket Books, 1978), p. 371.

2. George E. Vaillant, *The Natural History of Alcoholism* (Cambridge: Harvard University Press, 1983), pp. 311-312.

3. James R. Milam and Katherine Ketcham, *Under the Influence: A Guide to the Myths and Realities of Alcoholism* (New York: Bantam Books, 1981), pp. 32-33.

CHAPTER 13

1. Kurtz, Paul. *The Transcendental Temptation: A Critique of Religion and the Paranormal* (Buffalo, New York: Prometheus Books, 1986).

CHAPTER 17

1. National Institute on Alcohol Abuse and Alcoholism (NIAAA). *Fourth Special Report to the U.S. Congress on Alcohol and Health,* ed. John R. DeLuca, DGGS Pub. No. (ADM) 82-1080, 1981, p. 36.

2. Congress of the United States, Office of Technology Assessment. *Health Technology Case Study 22: The Effectiveness and Costs of Alcoholism Treatment,* prepared by Leonard Saxe, Ph.D., et al., OTA-HCS-22, 1983, p. 3.

3. NIAAA, Department of Biometry and Epidemiology, 1985, *Working Paper: Projections of Alcohol Abusers, 1980, 1985, 1990,* prepared by John Noble, pp. 5 and 6.

4. NIAAA, *Fifth Special Report to the U.S. Congress on Alcohol and Health,* from the Secretary of Health and Human Services, DHHS Publication No. (ADM) 84-1291, 1983, p.xiii.

5. R.T. Ravenholt, M.D., *Addiction Mortality in the U.S.,* National Institute on Drug Abuse (NIDA), March 1983.

6. Research Triangle Institute (RTI), *Economic Costs to Society of Alcohol and Drug Abuse and Mental Illness: 1980,* Henrick J. Harwood, et al., June 1984, pp. G-16 and 7.

7. (NIAAA), *Alcoholism Treatment Impact on Total Health Care Utilization and Costs,* U.S. Dept. of Health and Human Services, February 1985, pp. 1, 3.

8. Ravenholt, *Addiction Mortality,* NIDA, March 1983.

9. P. Regans, ABC News/Washington Post Poll, Survey #0190, May 1985.

10. NIAAA, *Fifth Special Report,* p. xv.

11. Children of Alcoholics Foundation, *Children of Alcoholics: A Review of the Literature,* 1985, Introduction and p. 2.

12. NIAAA, *Fifth Special Report,* p. 22.

13. NIAAA, *Third Special Report to the U.S. Congress on Alcohol and Health,* 1978, p. 14.

14. Nancy P. Gordon and Alfred McAlister. "Adolescent Drinking: Issues and Research," in *Promoting Adolescent Health* (New York: Academic Press, 1982), pp. 201, 203, 210. David W. Brook and Judith S. Brook, "Adolescent Alcohol Use," Editorial, *Alcohol and Alcoholism,* Vol. 20., No. 3 (Great Britain, 1985). p. 259.

15. Dorothy G. Singer, "Alcohol, Television and Teenagers," *Sex, Drugs, Rock 'N' Roll,* Yale University Family Television Research Consultation Center (New Haven: 1985), pp. 668, 671.

16. NIAAA, *Fifth Special Report*, p. 125.

17. Weekly Reader Publications, "A Study of Children's Attitudes and Perceptions about Drugs and Alcohol," conducted by the *Weekly Reader*, Xerox Education Publications, 1983, Table 2.

18. New York State Division of Alcoholism and Alcohol Abuse, *Drug and Alcohol Survey*, 1983.

19. NIAAA, *Fifth Special Report*, p. xiii.

20. RTI, *Economic Costs to Society*, p. B-3.

21. General Service Office of Alcoholics Anonymous, Inc., Membership Survey, 1983.

22. National Highway Traffic Safety Administration, *Alcohol in Fatally Injured Drivers*—1984, Washington, D.C.

23. National Highway Traffic Safety Administration, U.S. Dept. of Transportation, *Drunk Driving Facts.* National Center for Statistics and Analysis, June 1984.

24. *Health, United States,* 1980, National Center for Health Statistics, Public Health Service, U.S. DHHS Pub, No. (PHS) 81-1232, December 1980.

25. NIAAA, *Alcohol Health and Research World,* Summer 1985, Vol. 9, No. 4, p. 25.

26. NIAAA, *Alcohol Health and Research World,* Summer 1985, p. 28.

27. NIAAA, *Fifth Special Report,* pp. xix and xx.

28. NIAAA, *Fifth Special Report,* p. xx.

29. Bureau of Justice, Statistics Survey. 1983.

30. NIAAA, *Alcohol Health and Research World,* Spring 1984, Vol. 8, NO. 3, pp. 4 and 6.